2011

Gail

Happy Mother's
Day from one
Grandma to another (mama)!
Enjoy this on your porch
with a nice cup of coffee!

Love
Diane & Kaitlyn

*Stories, sayings, and scriptures to Encourage and Inspire*

# BIG
# hugs®
## for
## Grandmas

## Chrys Howard

Personalized Scriptures by
## LeAnn Weiss

**HOWARD BOOKS**
A DIVISION OF SIMON & SCHUSTER
New York   London   Toronto   Sydney

Our purpose at Howard Books is to:

> *Increase faith* in the hearts of growing Christians
> *Inspire holiness* in the lives of believers
> *Instill hope* in the hearts of struggling people everywhere

Because He's coming again!

**HOWARD**
BOOKS

Published by Howard Books, a division of Simon & Schuster, Inc.
1230 Avenue of the Americas, New York, NY 10020
www.howardpublishing.com

*Hugs for Grandma* © 2001 by Chrys Howard
*Hugs for Granddaughters* © 2005 by Chrys Howard

ISBN-13: 978-1-4165-4185-1
ISBN-10:    1-4165-4185-3

10 9 8 7 6 5 4 3 2 1

HOWARD and colophon are registered trademarks of Simon & Schuster, Inc.

Manufactured in the United States of America

For information regarding special discounts for bulk purchases, please contact: Simon & Schuster Special Sales at 1-800-456-6798 or business@simonandschuster.com.

Personalized scriptures by LeAnn Weiss, owner of Encouragement Company,
3006 Brandywine Dr., Orlando, FL 32806; 407-898-4410

*Hugs for Grandma*
Edited by Philis Boultinghouse
Interior design by LinDee Loveland

*Hugs for Granddaughters*
Edited by Between the Lines
Interior design by Stephanie D. Walker
Photography by Chrys Howard

Scripture quotations are taken from the *Holy Bible, New International Version* © 1973, 1978, 1984 International Bible Society. Used by permission of Zondervan; and the *Holy Bible, New King James Version* © 1982 by Thomas Nelson, Inc.

# hugs

_Stories, sayings, and scriptures to Encourage and Inspire_

## for
## Grandma

CHRYS HOWARD

Personalized Scriptures by
LEANN WEISS

*I love you!*

I dedicate this book to my grandmothers,
*Myrtle Anne Durham* and *Lela May Shackelford,*
who inspired, encouraged, and entertained me throughout my childhood.

I thank God for my mother, *Betty Jo Shackelford,*
and my mother-in-law, *Mamie Jean Howard,*
who did the same for my children.

Now, I pray that I will pass on the legacy of loving unconditionally
to my grandchildren, who make each day an adventure.
*John Luke, Sadie, Macy, Asa, Ally,*
*Will, Maddox, Aslyn, Bella,* and *Aevin—*

I love you!

# Contents

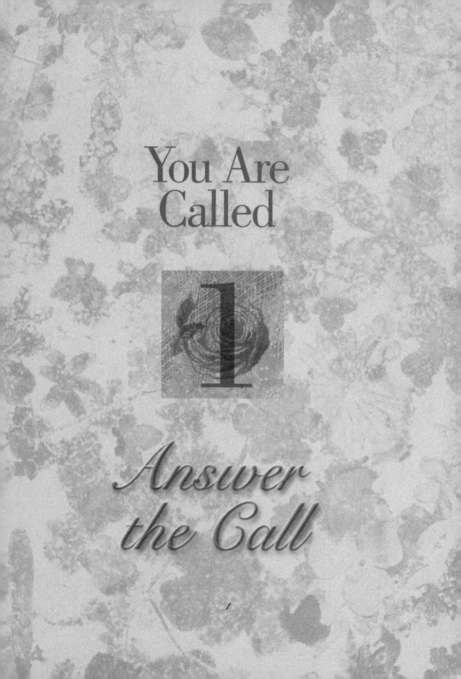

# You Are Called

# 1

# *Answer the Call*

$\mathcal{I}$'ve redeemed you and called you by name. I'll never abandon you in your search for Me. My name is 100 percent trustworthy. I love to do far beyond all that you can ask or dream according to My power, which is at work in your family even when you don't realize it.

Dreaming for you,

*Your God of Abundant Life*

—from Isaiah 43:1; Psalm 9:10; Ephesians 3:20

*Grandmothers,* thank you for being flexible about your "grandma" name.

Grandmothers are among the few people on earth who are content to be called anything someone else decides. People are fairly picky about their names, aren't they? No one likes to see her name misspelled in print. We cringe when we hear it mispronounced. We roll our eyes when we are called by someone else's name.

The dictionary tells us that a name is that by which a person or thing is designated. Psychologists tell us that calling someone by his or her name builds self-esteem and gives a feeling of importance. Schoolteachers tell us that they strive to learn their students' names quickly in order to help each child feel special and noticed. Children tell us it bothers them when their parents can't remember their names, listing the whole family before their own name is called.

But, grandmothers, you have risen above the name game. You have learned a great lesson from Jesus—Messiah, Lamb of God, Son of Man, Lord. Do you recognize these names? Of course you do. They are the names used to call on our Savior, Jesus. Each name contributes something unique and conjures up a different image or perspective of Jesus. And there are many more names for this one man, Jesus. Jesus invites us to call on his name often—in times of joy and in times of sorrow—and he never tires of hearing our calls.

What do your grandchildren call you? I would suspect that whatever it is, you are thrilled with it. I'm sure something special happened when you became Mimi, Nana, G-Mom, or Mamaw. Maybe it was something you said or did, or maybe it was just the name that past generations in your family have used. In any case, you each have your own story. And, just like Jesus, you don't really mind which name you are called.

Your grandchildren could call you anything, and you would answer. You are that special person who will always answer when they call, always listen when they speak, and always love them no matter what they do. You are their grandmother. And just like Jesus, you invite them to call on you whenever they want, and you will never tire of hearing your name.

*Just when a mother thinks her work is done, she becomes a grandmother.*

—Caroline Brownlow

*Being a mother was what Stacy wanted
most in her life.*

# An Answered Prayer

At some point in Stacy's life, she began dreaming of becoming a mother. She couldn't really remember when it began or what caused the desire to be so great. She suspected that it was because she was an only child and there weren't many "available" babies for her to play with. Her mother had said she was a natural nurturer, and taking care of others came easily to her.

Sometimes her mother had wished Stacy weren't so caring. Cats and dogs and little pink pigs all made their way into Stacy's heart. And because Stacy was an only child with no hope of siblings, her mom generally said yes to every animal she wanted. Although she wanted to draw the line after she found Stacy bathing the pig in her bathtub, she didn't. Friends called their house a "zoo for a day."

But being a mother was what Stacy wanted most in her life. She had longed to feel the soft, tender touch of her own baby's hand, to change diapers and make bottles. Her friends used to say, "Stacy, get a life. You don't want to do that stuff until you have to!" They didn't understand. Stacy really thought she was ready. Even her mother didn't understand. She and her mother had always had a close relationship, until that terrible day.

Stacy had tried to keep it a secret. Young girls just didn't have babies out of wedlock during the sixties. Well, of course they *did*. But no one knew it. Everything was kept quiet. Girls were suddenly

sent off to visit relatives in California or sent away to "summer camp." Even if someone suspected the truth, no one talked about it. Although it is just as wrong to have sex outside of marriage today as it was in the sixties, people today seem more understanding and supportive of the choices a young girl might make. Back then, it was out of the question to have a baby and not be married. Raising a child alone was rarely considered.

"Stacy, this decision is for your good, sweetheart. You're only sixteen. You have your whole life ahead of you." Her mother had said those words through tears and sobs so violent that Stacy was afraid her mother would never stop. "You can't take care of a baby. You have no job, no education. What would you do?" And her mom just kept quoting a scripture in Proverbs about trusting God. At the time, Stacy wasn't sure whom to trust. The advice she kept hearing wasn't what she wanted to hear.

But Stacy really had no choice. It was the late sixties, and even though the world was in a sexual revolution, her parents were not. And neither was the rest of her family. There was nothing to do except put the baby up for adoption.

As Stacy grew up and older, she eventually came to terms with her mother's inability to make things better. But at the time, she couldn't understand her mother. This woman had always "fixed" everything for her, but she couldn't fix this.

The day Stacy signed the adoption papers was the saddest day of her life. Her mother had to hold her hand to steady it so she could get her signature on the appropriate line. Her eyes were so heavy and so tired from crying, she could barely see what she was writing. She had prayed that it was only a bad dream and that she would soon wake up.

But it wasn't a dream. *How could one night cause such pain? How could I have been so foolish? I thought Jeff truly loved me and would always be there for me!* Stacy learned a valuable lesson in one night: Appearances can be deceiving.

*So much has happened since that day,* Stacy thought. But Stacy was as nervous today as she had been thirty-two years ago. Only this time, it was a "happy" nervous. She was on her way to meet her baby girl. She knew she wasn't a baby anymore, but she couldn't help but think of her that way—she had no other memories of her. She hoped new memories would soon be made.

## An Answered Prayer

When the phone rang exactly three weeks, one day, and six hours ago, Stacy knew the missing piece of her "life puzzle" was being nudged into place. Her life puzzle had been almost perfect; she would never deny that. Her husband, Kevin, had loved and supported her for twenty-eight years. She had worked for many years in local Christian ministries, and in the past ten years, she had spoken openly about the baby girl she had given up. She had counseled countless young girls in the same situation. Well, she always hesitated to say "the same" because every situation is unique. Certainly the times have changed, and young women have more options today. But that's one reason Stacy decided to be more vocal. She never wanted abortion to be one of those options. Even though she didn't get to raise her baby, she cherished the thought that she was alive and growing and clung to the hope of their reunion.

Although Stacy had many happy times in her life, there was a very sad part. She and Kevin had never had a child. Her desire and dream to be a mother had never become a reality.

## You Are Called—*Answer the Call*

Although she had lots of "babies," as she always referred to her kindergarten students, Stacy never again felt the touch of her own newborn—not since March 13, 1968, when she kissed her baby girl good-bye.

Stacy knew she was a great teacher. Year after year parents requested her classroom for their children. And she knew she had impacted so many little lives. And she trusted God. She wasn't going to be bitter. But there were days, she had to admit, when she wanted to know why. *Why couldn't I have another baby?*

*Road construction for the next four miles. Don't they realize I've got a baby to meet! Of course they don't! Life just keeps going on. I'm seeing my baby for the first time in thirty-two years, and the road still has to be fixed! And bills must be paid, yards must be mowed, and a million other significantly insignificant things have to happen. But*

*nothing will come between my child and me…this time.*

Stacy saw a small, neat, white frame house. The yard had been freshly mowed, and the garden was full of new petunias— all waiting to welcome company. Flowing softly in the breeze were pink balloons that Stacy later discovered numbered thirty-two—one for each year Stacy and her baby had been separated. She pulled into the driveway, turned off the engine, put the car in park, and automatically began praying. *Dear God, thank you for this day. Bless us and grant us peace as we begin this new relationship.*

As her eyes opened, so did the door of the house. Out stepped Jenna—the most beautiful young woman she had ever seen. Trembling, Stacy managed to get out of the car. It was an experience she knew she would hardly be able to describe to her husband. He had elected to stay at home so her emotions could be hers alone. With every part of her body, she felt as she had felt when she gave birth to this little girl. Not the pain part—just the love part. How she had wanted her! How she had cried when she knew she couldn't keep her. How she had struggled each year just to get through March 13, knowing her child was blowing out candles and opening presents, and she would never see her do those things.

The reunion was going perfectly—pictures had been exchanged, and hugs had been given until their arms hurt. Stacy was realistic and knew that some tough times would come. Questions must be asked, and answers must be given. But for today, so far, everything was perfect. And the best part was meeting Micah and Meagen, her grandchildren. She was a grandmother!

When Jenna had told her over the phone that she had grandchildren, a new set of tears began to flow. *Finally a baby to cuddle!* Actually, Jenna had told Stacy that her children were the reason she had tracked Stacy down. Jenna's adoptive mother had died of ovarian cancer three years earlier, and Jenna longed for her children to have the love of a grandmother. But truth be known, Jenna also longed for the love of a mother. Someone to share pictures with and have lunch with. Someone to share her life with. Finding her birth mother seemed the perfect solution.

Stacy couldn't have been happier when Jenna finally said the words Stacy had waited so long to hear: "Can I call you Mama?"

"Yes," came Stacy's quick reply. "I've waited so long to hear you say that word!" Jenna picked up

Micah, who had just turned two. Meagen, only six months old, had already snuggled up to her new grandmother.

"Micah, I want you to know that this is my mama, and that she is your grandmother—yours and Meagen's," Stacy said softly.

Micah's two-year-old brain went to work, and he quickly responded: "If she's your mama, then she's my two-mama!"

Jenna laughed and explained, "Ever since I had Meagen, I've said so many times how I have two babies. Now he thinks he's met another mama. We can work on another grandmother name if you want us to."

"Of course not! It's perfect. As a matter of fact, I can't wait to share this with my friends."

After all these years of waiting to be a mama, Stacy was delighted to be someone's "two-mama." All of her friends who were now grandparents had spent hours deciding what they wanted their grandchildren to call them, and this little guy had figured out Stacy's name in one

minute. Stacy had never heard it used before. She knew her friends would be jealous of such a special name. "I wonder if it's legal to copyright a name?" she joked to Jenna.

*Appearances certainly can be deceiving,* Stacy thought, as she drove away from the little white house with thirty-two pink balloons. *I began this day as Stacy—no children, but now I'm Stacy—Jenna's mama and Meagen and Micah's two-mama. What a double blessing!*

*"Trust in the Lord with all your heart and lean not on your own understanding." Thank you, God, for answering my prayers, and thank you, Mom, for reminding me often of that scripture.*

*What special memories do you have of being*
*"called" by your grandchildren?*

_____

_____

_____

_____

_____

_____

_____

_____

_____

_____

# You Have
# a Gift

# Give It

*Y*ou're a special part of My family, sharing My treasures. Be a faithful steward of everything I've entrusted to you. When you give, you'll bountifully receive beyond your initial gift. Remember, love is the gift that holds everything together in perfect unity.

Extravagantly,

*Your God of Every Good and Perfect Gift*

—from Romans 8:17; 1 Corinthians 4:2; Luke 6:38; Colossians 3:14; James 1:17

*Grandmothers* are notorious for wanting to lavish gifts on their grandchildren. Lavishing gifts on a grandchild is a grandmother's right, many would say. But there is the question of "spoiling" them. A wise grandmother once said, "It's not what you give a child that spoils them; it's what you allow them to do with it that does the damage."

Even so, you must remember that the greatest gifts are not bought at Toys"R"Us. They aren't found on the shopping channel, and you can't charge them on your MasterCard. Oh, bicycles and baby dolls are nice. But there is something more precious and actually more costly.

Do you realize that the future of homemade biscuits rests with you? Only you have the secret knowledge of knowing where to look for a rainbow after the rain has stopped. And then there's the ability to decide what size container will best hold a lizard, a frog, and four leaves. And who knows better than a grandmother how to rock a baby to sleep or to fold a blanket to custom fit a tiny newborn?

And the best gift of all is your ability to love unconditionally.

Grandmothers, your age and wisdom have taught you to love with expectations but without conditions. You can look at the face of a grandchild and not see a dirty-faced kid with too much energy; rather, you see the future. Your vision is sharpening with age. "When others see a shepherd boy, God may see a king," so the song by Ray Boltz goes. You, like God, see the potential, yet you do not apply the pressure. You are content to watch as if waiting for that first flower to bloom in spring, knowing that the bloom will come in time.

These are the best gifts, aren't they? What's the price? Maybe a Saturday morning when homemade biscuits are ordered by hungry teens or a summer evening waiting for the rain to stop. Perhaps it will cost you much-needed sleep when you are assigned late-night duty tending a fussy newborn.

Most of all, it will cost you your heart, given to those you love the most. There's not a grandchild alive who wouldn't want to receive these gifts. So go ahead! Lavish all you want. Your gifts will reap eternal rewards!

© Photography by Lamar

*The best gifts are tied
with heartstrings.*

—Jo Petty

The instructions for the grandkids had been
to arrive at midnight with ladders,
decorations, and glue guns.

# The Gift

*Okay, I'm almost seventy,* Betty sighed, as she locked the office door for the evening, *and I'm feeling every minute of it.* Betty Shackelford, a strong woman, whose Southern manners would never allow her to show her problems, was just plain tired! Although she couldn't understand how her mother's picture got on her new driver's license, she actually looked great for sixty-eight and enjoyed good health.

But three years ago, at a time when her friends were retiring and relaxing, Betty and her husband of forty-five years decided to open a real-estate business. So Betty became the office manager.

## You Have a Gift—*Give It*

Just as they had hoped, the business flourished. Betty's job was very demanding, and when she wasn't too tired, she sometimes snickered a little and patted herself on the back at the thought that she'd never worked a day in her life until she was sixty-five years old. Well, outside the home, that is!

After all, she had raised six kids. There was bound to be some management experience in that job. As a matter of fact, Betty really looked at managing the business office just as she had her home: "Stay on a schedule, and do everything in love" was her motto. So far, it had worked.

But as Betty closed the office that particular night, she was even too tired to go to her grandson, Jake's, basketball game. And that wasn't like Betty. It was Jake's senior year, and she never missed a game. But tonight she just couldn't make it.

Betty knew the phone would be ringing about the time she dozed off to sleep, so she willed herself to read one more page as she waited, patiently. *It's great to have so much family around,* she thought, *but you can't get away with any-*

*thing.* And sure enough, just before ten o'clock, the first phone call came.

"Mom, you okay?" her oldest daughter asked. "You weren't at the game."

"I'm just a little tired," was the reply. "I guess with the office work and trying to get ready for Christmas, I overdid it a little. I'll be all right tomorrow." She repeated her story three more times as kids and grandkids called to check on "Mamaw."

*Now for some much-needed sleep,* Betty thought as she closed her eyes. But rest escaped her. She mentally went through the checklist for the next day: Get the new house listings to the newspaper; take pictures of the house on Lakeland Drive; take a shower gift by Joneal's house; go to Jake's next game; decorate the office.

*Decorate the office! Now that's something I really don't have time to do!* She almost cried as a feeling of being totally overwhelmed engulfed her. "No, I can do it," she said out loud.

"What's wrong?" said her husband, Luther, who was awakened from a peaceful sleep.

"Oh nothing, go back to sleep," Betty said. "I was just working on tomorrow."

## You Have a Gift—*Give It*

"Why don't you work on tomorrow when tomorrow gets here?" Luther replied as he rolled over and went back to sleep.

*Easy for you to say,* Betty thought. *What was that little phrase my mother used to say, "A woman's work is never..."?* She finally fell asleep.

The next morning, Betty was ready to tackle the day. Well, mentally she was. But her back didn't feel right. She must have pulled something when she picked up Sadie the day before. Her granddaughter, Korie, had surprised her at the office with her two-year-old daughter, Sadie. Betty and Sadie had become best buddies. Sadie's deep dimples, dark brown eyes, and bubbling personality made her a great-grandmother's dream, and she loved to run and jump into Mamaw's waiting arms.

"I may have to hold off on decorating the office," Betty told Luther. "I seem to have pulled a muscle. I think Sadie has put on a pound or two."

"No problem," said Luther. "You'll get it done."

*Easy for you to say,* Betty thought.

Betty finished getting ready for work and was out the door by seven-thirty. She had just a few stops she wanted to make before she headed to the office. She knew that once she got there, she probably wouldn't get to leave until dark. *Thank goodness Wal-Mart never closes. How did we ever get our errands run before all-night shopping?* Betty wondered. Another stop for gas, and Betty was off to work.

She rounded the corner of Thomas and Arkansas Road, thankful that she lived in a small town. Many days Betty thought that if she had to fight big-city traffic, it might be enough to put her over that pro-verbial "edge."

As Betty pulled into the parking lot of Shackelford-French Real Estate, she was shocked to see that even in broad daylight, white twinkle lights sparkled on the bushes that surrounded her office. The tall white columns that seemed to guard the front door had been transformed into giant candy canes. Wreaths had been placed in each window, and a "Have a Merry Christmas" welcome mat warmed the entrance.

Betty slowly got out of her car. Her eyes were as bright as a child's on Christmas morning, and her hands flew to cover her mouth. She carefully opened the front door and was greeted by a small, fully decorated Christmas tree, a basket filled with candy canes, and a card that read, "Mamaw, we hope you enjoy this holiday surprise. Thank you for always making Christmas special for us. We love you, your grandchildren."

Betty had not realized that Korie had come by the office the day before to "case the joint," as she later told her. She had been hard at work organizing her brothers, sisters, and cousins to give a gift that she knew her mamaw truly needed.

The instructions for the grandkids had been to arrive at midnight with ladders, decorations, and glue guns. Two hours and many laughs later, the gift was finished, and nine very excited grandchildren drove away and eagerly waited for the phone calls to come the next day.

Betty was touched almost beyond words. But she managed to leave nine messages that day that said, "Thank you, my grandchildren. There's not a better gift you could have given me."

And for some reason, Betty's back didn't seem to bother her so much that day.

*Record for future generations a special memory of a gift-giving or gift-receiving time with your grandchildren.*

_____

_____

_____

_____

_____

_____

_____

_____

_____

_____

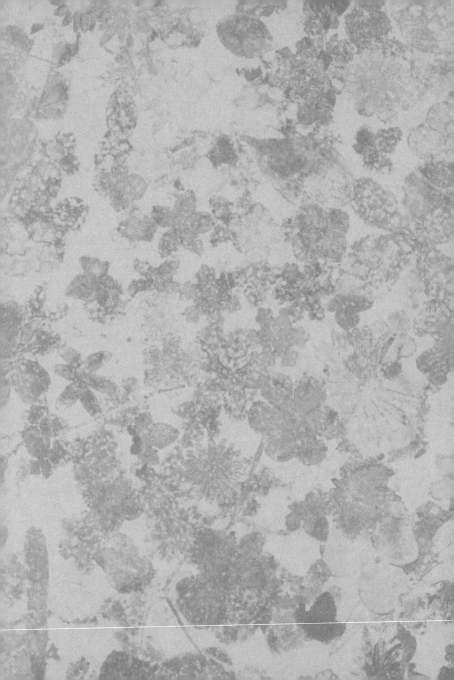

# You Are a
# Cheerleader

Keep
Cheering

© Photography by Lamar

*Y*our words have amazing, life-giving power! Encourage your loved ones and build them up daily as you each run with endurance the race I've custom-tailored for you. Remember, I'm your rest stop, surrounding you with victory songs! You can do all things because I strengthen you. Even failure can't separate you from My unconditional love for you.

Rooting for you,
*Your God*

—from Proverbs 18:21;
1 Thessalonians 5:11;
Hebrews 12:1–3; Psalm 32:7;
Philippians 4:13; Romans 8:35

*Have you read* Hebrews 12 lately? Go ahead, read it. What better visual image could there be than the thunderous roar of a crowd cheering a runner on to victory? And the great news is that it's more than a visual image—it's reality! The Hebrews writer states: "Therefore, since we are surrounded by such a great cloud of witnesses, let us throw off everything that hinders and the sin that so easily entangles, and let us run with perseverance the race marked out for us." As a grandmother, you understand the race the Hebrews writer was talking about—the race of life. Perhaps you're right in the middle of it, or maybe you're nearing the end. In any case, you understand. When Hebrews 12 was written, the readers needed encouragement to stay strong in the face of persecution. They were called to follow the perfect example of Jesus. To encourage them, the Hebrews writer told them that many, many had gone before them and were cheering them on to victory.

While you certainly don't face the same kind or degree of persecution faced during biblical days, you do realize the difficulties and joys involved in completing the race. And we all need encouragement, don't we? We all need someone to cheer us on— someone who has already been there, right where we are now—someone who has crossed the finish line! Those who've run the race before you know your struggles, they understand the sacrifices you make, and they can truly feel your pain.

Grandmas, your grandchildren are just entering the race. And it's a race that is bigger than the Olympics, more strenuous than a Grand Slam event, and more challenging than the Super Bowl. They're entering the race of life, and they need a cheerleader. That's where you come in. You, like the witnesses in Hebrews, have already run the laps they are just beginning. You're still running, of course, but many, many laps are under your belt. New college roommates, first dates, job interviews— been there, done that, haven't you?

So, now, cheer them on. Give them advice. Encourage them to stay strong. Support their activities. Two bits, four bits, six bits, a dollar—come on, Grandma, stand up and holler!

*Consistent, timely encouragement has the staggering magnetic power to draw an immortal soul to the God of hope. The One whose name is Wonderful Counselor.*

—Charles R. Swindoll

*Statistics aside, she had the desire to win. Everyone was convinced she would be the state champion.*

# A True Champion

"A champion is one who gets up when he can't." Those words were burned into Katelyn's mind as if someone had etched them in with a wood-burning kit at summer camp. The words were on a poster her grandmother had given her in the ninth grade. Katelyn had placed the poster at the foot of her bed, and for the past four years, she had started and ended her day with that challenge. How would Katelyn hold up when faced with a real challenge? Would she be a true champion?

There was no doubt in her grandmother's mind that she was. Grandma Jo had been there for her at every single track meet—all the way back to her second-grade track-and-field day. It didn't matter where the meet was held, Grandma Jo was always there. "Everybody's got to be somewhere," she would say. And Grandma Jo would hop in the car and drive two hours to Katelyn's school. Grandma Jo would sit up in the bleachers, wearing her big, floppy hat to shield her face from the sun. Grandma Jo had spent her teen years in southern California and never missed a chance to tell her grandchildren that too much sun was responsible for her wrinkles. She was the epitome of grace and poise—the dignified grandmother. At least until Katelyn reached the finish line. Then dignity and grace went out the window. She would jump for joy, hugging everyone in the stands. Next, she would run down to the track and give Katelyn the biggest hug, telling her she was so

proud of her. She would say, "Katelyn, you have a gift! A gift for running."

And she was right. Running came easily to Katelyn. Like someone who sings with perfect pitch or plays the piano by ear, Katelyn could run. So she did. But as she got older, the coaches required more and more of her. By the ninth grade, she was having to train after school and on weekends. Hours of running and weight training took the place of playing, practices crowded out parties, and healthy food replaced junk food.

After a particularly formidable workout on a day when the temperature was in the nineties, Katelyn called her grandmother. "Grandma Jo," she cried, "I wish God had given me a talent I didn't have to work so hard at!"

But Grandma Jo gently reminded her that God didn't have any talents like that. "We all have to work at whatever talent God gives us, or it will be taken away," she said. "Remember the parable of the talents?" Of course, Katelyn remembered the parable, but she had never thought of it like that.

A few days later, Katelyn received the poster in the mail that was to become her symbol of strength. The poster showed six runners, each straining to be the first to reach the finish tape. Veins clearly being challenged, muscles pushed to a new level, and teeth clenched as each face revealed a passionate desire to win. It was just the challenge Katelyn needed. She set her sights higher, and her goals became clearer.

Blue ribbons, red ribbons, trophies, and medals began to fill her room. Victory after victory, her grandmother was there to congratulate and cheer her on. Time seemed to fly by until, one day during her senior year of high school, she found herself at the state track meet. All the hard work would pay off here.

Katelyn had run only hurdles for the past two years, but was seemingly made for the event. Statistically speaking, she was the district and regional champion and came into the state meet with the second fastest time. Statistics aside, she had the desire to win. Everyone was convinced she would be the state champion.

Every athlete has his or her pre-sport rituals. Katelyn was down on the track going through her predetermined set: Bounce three or four times, shake out arms and legs, touch toes, and then look into the crowd for support. There was her whole family— Mom, Dad, brothers, sisters, aunts, uncles, and of course, her Grandma Jo. She had driven nine hours to see this important event. She wouldn't have missed it for anything. It was late May in southern Louisiana, and the "track" hat, as Katelyn called it, was shading her face. She was poised and ready to hug and congratulate. She gave Katelyn one last wave for good luck.

Katelyn bent down to the spongy red track and spread her fingers out in precisely the same way she had done a hundred times. Then she placed her toes snugly into the starting block. She, like the crowd, waited for the familiar sound of the gun. Then the official yelled, "Everyone up!" Shaking out her arms and legs, Katelyn was determined to stay focused. Back down they all went. Every finger in the perfect spot, toes lined up, head lowered, Katelyn was ready. Once again, the official called for everyone to get up. Back up and once again, back down. Surely, the gun would go off this time. But it was not to be. Even the crowd was getting nervous as once again the official asked the runners to stand. This time he told Katelyn to move her block back. *What could be wrong?* Katelyn thought. It was where

she always put it. Although puzzled, she was ready for the race to begin, so she did as she was told. She felt an uneasy feeling in her stomach. She thought of her grandma's last wave, and she knew it meant "You can do it." So with new resolve, she calmly stretched out her fingers as if playing a piano piece at Christmas, and waited. Finally, the sound of the gun. They were off. She had a great start and seemed to fly over the first hurdle. But her toe skimmed the second hurdle. The third hurdle shook as once again her foot lightly touched it. On the fourth hurdle, she was down. The crowd went instantly silent in disbelief. Katelyn felt their sadness for her as a dream had quickly died. The other runners flew past her. There was no reason for them to stop. Nobody blamed them.

Katelyn's knee was badly cut and her hands were burned from rubbing across the track. But she knew

it was time for the real test. Was her grandmother's poster to become a reality? Could she get up and complete this race? She began the long journey to the finish line. What usually took less than sixteen seconds seemed like an eternity.

## A True Champion

The audience applauded her determination as Katelyn made it to the finish line and quietly walked off the track. She knew there would be no medals, no articles in the paper, no congratulatory hugs. And she felt so sorry for those who had traveled so far . . . only to be disappointed. As she raised her head, there came her family with Grandma Jo leading the way. Everyone who had stood by her in victory now stood beside her in defeat.

But was it a defeat? Grandma Jo hadn't traveled nine hours just to see Katelyn win; she came to see her finish a race. And just like God, she was just as ready to wrap her arms around the runner who had hit a few hurdles, suffered some scrapes, and finished last as she was the runner who cleared every hurdle and finished first. As Grandma Jo tells the story, on that day, she saw a champion run a race, and Katelyn came to understand more clearly the love of God.

*Tell the story of when you cheered on a grandchild during a challenging time.*

_____

_____

_____

_____

_____

_____

_____

_____

_____

_____

_____

# You Are a
# Forever Student

4

*Keep
Learning*

$\mathcal{N}$ot even old age, wrinkles, or gray hairs can stop Me from sustaining you. Don't lose heart! Your external appearances may be fading away, but I'm renewing your spirit day by day. May you always speak with wisdom and faithful instruction.

Teaching you,

*Your God of Wisdom*

—from Isaiah 46:4; 2 Corinthians 4:16; Proverbs 31:26

*Chances are* you haven't heard a school bell ring in years, but the shrill sound of any bell probably brings back memories of a small wooden desk and a teacher with a stern look. Do you ever wish the final bell would ring and school would be out forever?

The reality is that school is still in session, but you'll be happy to hear that you won't forever be waiting for a school bus or a car-pool. And you can now pass up the clean, white notebooks and freshly sharpened pencils that complete the "Back to School" displays at Wal-Mart and Kmart. And the worries you had with locker combinations, lunch money, and best friends have discreetly faded just like the yearbook pages they are recorded on.

Yes, the physical description of your schoolroom has vastly changed, as well as the physical description of your teacher. But the opportunities to learn are ever present. Grandmothers, those opportunities will present quite a challenge to you—you'll have to apply yesterday's wisdom to today's challenges! And who better to present those challenges to you than your grandchildren?

You've lived long enough to realize that the best teachers are not always those who are old and wise or hold a fancy degree. Your grandchildren will supply you with enough material to fill a three-ring binder with five divider tabs. You've never had a professor who could talk as fast as a four-year-old grandson or with as much emotion as a twelve-year-old granddaughter. They will gently remind you when hairstyles change and rock groups go out of style. They will push you harder than any PE teacher with words like "Run, Grandma!" or "Can you still ride a bike?"

Yes, your grandchildren will be full of valuable information and insight. Now, what do you have to do? Just study hard and try to pass their tests! You can do it, Grandma!

*Cheerfulness and content are
great beautifiers and are famous
preservers of youthful looks.*

—Charles Dickens

*Today was her birthday, and she planned to see a plastic surgeon on the following Thursday afternoon.*

# Wrinkles and Rainbows

Flipping on the light to her makeup mirror, Andrea began the process of getting ready for the day. Foundation, eyeliner, blush, lipstick—just the basics. "Don't go out without your face," her mama used to say. Wearing makeup wasn't a matter of vanity; it was simply viewed as appropriate. It was putting your best foot forward. After all, they were ladies of the South.

Southern women always looked their best: peaches-and-cream complexions; natural, but fixed hairstyles; casual, but elegant clothing—that's a true Southern lady. Andrea's grandchildren often teased her when she wore white linen to their ball games. "Why are you so dressed up, Mama Andrea?" But Andrea would tell them white linen is not dressed up, just comfortable.

Andrea was a "cute" grandmother. She had a youthful appearance that included a modern, short hairdo—not "old lady" hair—that framed a small, round face. And she was petite. Anybody petite is labeled "cute" from early on. She had gotten used to that description. What she hadn't gotten used to was the skin on her cheeks becoming droopy. She wasn't sure if the word *droopy* was the medical term, but it certainly was accurate.

Today was her birthday, and she planned to see a plastic surgeon on the following Thursday afternoon. She had decided that at sixty-five, she could do something about her "droopies." She was so nervous

about the appointment that it took her weeks to get the courage to make it. Several of her friends had used this particular doctor and were pleased with the results.

## Wrinkles and Rainbows

As she sat in front of the makeup mirror, she moved the skin on her face around, trying to get a glimpse of what she might look like post-droopy. *What will Billy think about this?* she thought. *I wonder if he'll even notice.*

Billy was her first great-grandson, and every time she was with him, he would take his little fingers and pull the skin on her face. He did it so softly. It wasn't in any way a mean gesture. It was just his four-year-old way of touching and identifying her as his grandmother. *He probably won't notice. Anyway, this surgery is for me. Not anyone else. Just putting my best foot forward.*

Andrea finished her makeup session and headed to her closet to dress. She wasn't used to having so much time to dress and pamper herself. Her husband and children were doing all the cooking. She wasn't to do anything—her family had made that clear. No one wanted to celebrate at a restaurant, so the solution was for the family to share the cooking responsibilities. Andrea wanted to help, and would have been happy to, but they insisted.

## You Are a Forever Student—*Keep Learning*

*What do you wear to a birthday party when you're sixty-five years old?* It seemed to Andrea that it was just yesterday that she was deciding what to wear to her sixth birthday. Her mama had wanted her to wear a fancy party dress with white patent leather shoes. She had wanted to wear a new pair of blue gingham shorts with a matching shirt. Her mama finally convinced her that the party dress was more appropriate. *I wonder what Mama would think of the clothes my grandchildren will wear tonight? No doubt there will be an assortment of blue jeans and shorts. They will be precious, and no one will care what they have on. The times are so different.*

Andrea carefully selected a blue linen skirt, a freshly ironed white blouse, and white sandals with tiny flowers across the toe. She did have blue jeans in her closet, and she wore them, but not for a birthday party.

The meal was delicious. Andrea was surprised at the assortment of meats. Her husband had prepared his speciality: chicken, beef, and ribs marinated all night then grilled to perfection. He had really worked hard to make the evening special. The vegetables, salads, and desserts were compliments of her two daughters and one daughter-in-law. No restaurant in town would have had better food. And it was so nice to relax at home and enjoy the family without the distraction of others. That was the best part.

As the sun set, Andrea found herself in her favorite spot doing one of her most favorite things—sitting on the porch swing with Billy. He was adorable. His curly hair had just recently gotten its first "big boy" haircut, and his big brown eyes looked up at her like a little puppy dog. Billy had a gentle spirit—there was no other way to describe him—he was just born with it. He was one of those kids who laughs at everything and loves everyone.

Billy was chattering about playing baseball in the backyard with his daddy; he'd been working hard to learn how to hit the ball. Next year he would be five and could play T-ball. Andrea delighted in hearing these stories and anything else Billy wanted to tell her. Billy was getting sleepy and had laid his head down in Andrea's lap. Andrea looked down and smiled at this precious

child. "Billy, I can't wait until your first game. I'm going to be right there cheering you on."

Billy stared intently at Andrea and then said, "Mama Andrea, when you smile, your face makes rainbows."

Andrea laughed out loud. "My face makes rainbows! Billy, I just thought it made wrinkles. How fun to think that it makes rainbows! Thank you for telling me that."

Later that evening, as Andrea retold the story to her husband, he wanted to know if she was going to cancel her doctor's appointment. Andrea stared in the mirror and thought, *No, but I will tell him to leave enough for a rainbow.*

*What fresh view on life have
you learned from your grandchildren?*

_____

_____

_____

_____

_____

_____

_____

_____

_____

_____

_____

# You Have
# a Secret

# 5

## Share It

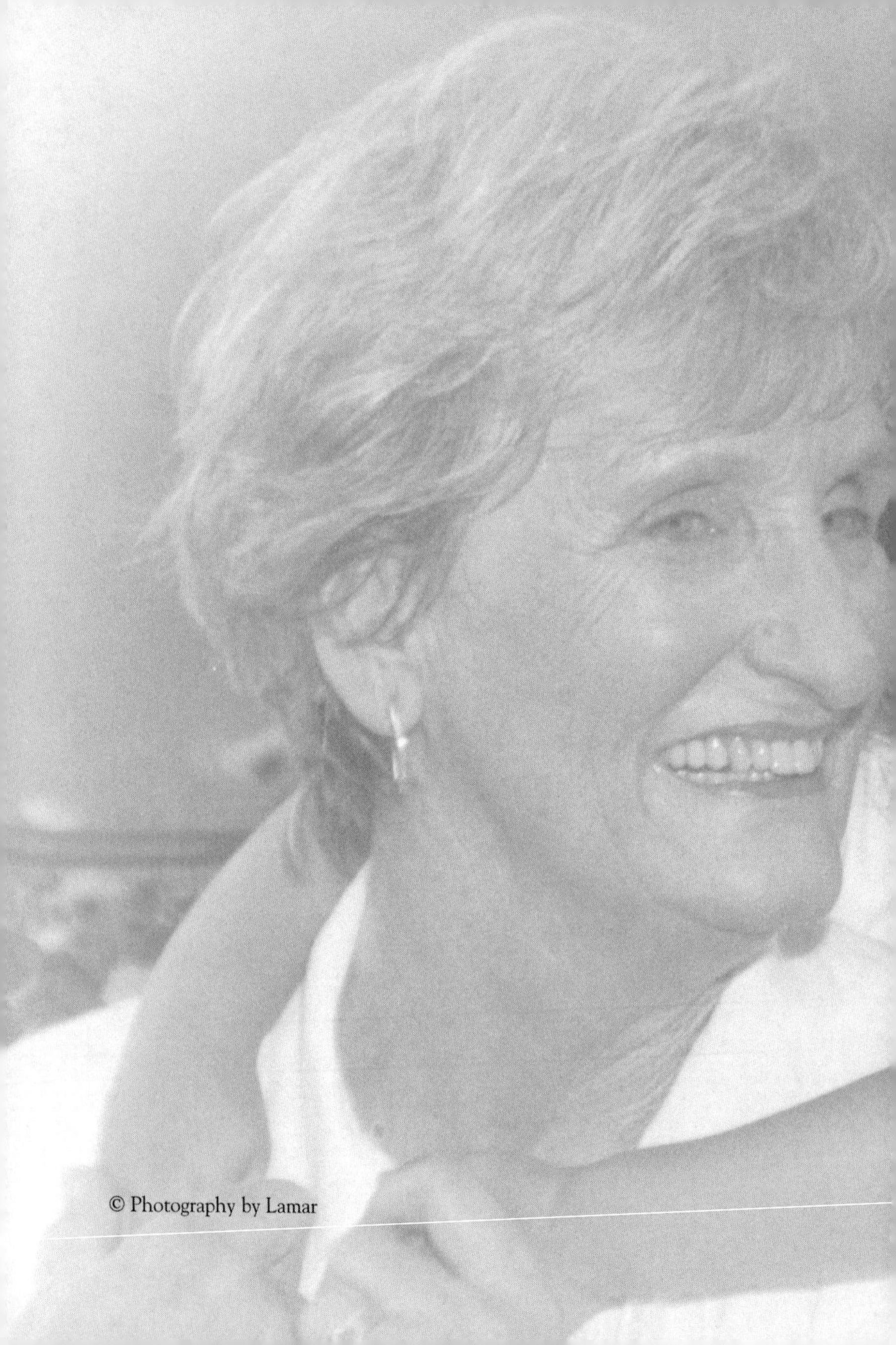

*I*'ve searched you and know you. The secret things in life belong to Me! But the treasures I've revealed to you belong to you and your family to be passed down for generations. And be patient—I'm not finished with you yet! I'm still in the process of completing the good work I started in you.

Intimately,

*Your Creator and God*

—from Psalm 139:1; Deuteronomy 29:29; Philippians 1:6

*Has it ever* been truer than today that grandmas come in all shapes and sizes? Like fresh fallen snowflakes that become a mountain of white, each grandmother is unique. Yes, some of you are still blonde, brunette, or redheaded, without a gray hair in sight (thanks, Clairol), and some retain a somewhat girlish figure (thanks, aerobics). More and more of us are still working outside the home, playing tennis, running in marathons, and climbing mountains.

But there are others who have slowed down a bit, acquired a beautiful head of white hair, and spend their time gardening, sewing, and canning. And there are many, many somewhere in-between. But, grandmas, while you may not look alike or act alike, there is one thing you all have in common: you are the mother of one of your grandchildren's parents. Oh, what a unique position that puts you in.

What childhood secrets are secured in your closets, drawers, and under your beds! You are the one who can look at your grandchild and say, "He acts just like his father" or, "She is the spitting image of her mother." And with this knowledge, you hold the invaluable ability to link the past to the present.

It doesn't matter whether you're forty-four or seventy-four, or whether you play golf on Saturdays or put up peas. It doesn't matter whether you live next door or a thousand miles away. You hold the key—that most important key that unlocks secrets of the past to a wide-eyed child—a child who never thought of his or her parents as children. Secrets that only someone who was there could know. When you think about it, Grandma, you, your husband, and God are the only people in your grandchildren's lives who witnessed the early years of their parents. And just as God, who knows us so well, realizes that deeper knowledge of a person brings understanding and love, you must recognize the power you hold to unite generations with a single story. So tell some stories—remind your children of their past, and let your grandchildren know that we were all young once.

*I want future generations to remember my good advice, but most of all I want them to remember my love.*

—Heather Whitestone

Each line and wrinkle represented a story in the life
of this sometimes "aggravating" little woman.

# Grandma Shack

"Mom, do I have to take her with me?" Jessica moaned through clenched teeth. "Every time she hears my keys jingle, she picks up her purse! I can't go anywhere without my grandmother!" Jessica had only been seven when her Grandma Shack moved in. At the time of the move, Grandma Shack wasn't feeble by any means. She wasn't sick. She wasn't really that old. There was just no point in her living alone. Nine years had passed, and she still wasn't that feeble or that old. And Jessica was right—she was always ready to go. But a sixteen-year-old with a new car doesn't want her grandmother riding shotgun everywhere she goes.

## You Have a Secret— *Share It*

"Mom, how did she get to be sixty-eight and not get a driver's license?"

Jessica's mom knew this was hard on Jessica. Actually, it had been hard on the whole family. When her mother-in-law had come to live with them, Jo wanted to make her feel welcome. But she had her six children to consider. Three very active boys and three equally active girls seemed to occupy every available inch of their four-bedroom home. Adding on to their house wasn't an option, so Grandma Shack had to share a room with Jessica, who was the youngest. Now that the older girls were in college, Jessica had moved into their room. Jo knew that over the years, the living arrangement had worked out fine, but she now felt some relief knowing her youngest daughter finally had some privacy.

There was no denying that Grandma Shack wasn't

easy to live with. She was quick to lay down some ground rules as she rooted out her place in the family nine years earlier. "There will be limited babysitting," this strong-willed, tiny Indian woman had said. Jo could still picture her standing there—all four feet eleven inches tall with stick-straight white hair and hands on her hips. "I raised my children; now you raise yours. And I won't clean up after anyone but myself. I did my share of that also. I don't mind sharing a room, but when my soap operas are on in the afternoon, I like it quiet."

Jo remembered how she joked to her husband, Luke, that Grandma Shack just might make them sign a contract. Once the move was complete, a trunk, a white wicker rocker, a small TV, and twenty shoeboxes with important papers now occupied one-half of Jessica's pink and white ruffled, little-girl bedroom. On more than one occasion, Jo wondered what she had gotten her family into.

"Jessica, just take her with you one more time. I'll talk to your daddy about her. Maybe he can talk to her about letting us know ahead of time when she needs an errand run," Jo pleaded with Jessica.

"Oh, all right," said Jessica. "Maybe I won't see anyone I know!"

"Grandma, I'm ready. Do you still need to pick up some things?" Jessica called down the hallway. There was not even a hint of disrespect in her voice. Jo and

## You Have a Secret—*Share It*

Luke had been determined to raise their children to respect their elders, even if they weren't happy with them at the moment.

All the children knew Grandma had sacrificed so much to raise her family. Her life had not been easy. Jo had often thought that Grandma's face was truly a road map of her life. Each line and wrinkle represented a story in the life of this sometimes "aggravating" little woman. A woman who struggled to raise six children after leaving an alcoholic and abusive husband. *How did she endure so much? Losing a son in a motorcycle accident, sending the four remaining sons off one by one to fight a war, seeing that each child received a proper education—all the time wondering how to put food on the table. Thank you, God, that my life is easier than Grandma's was*, Jo prayed.

Grandma Shack quickly grabbed her purse and followed her granddaughter out the door. Jessica looked back at her mom and rolled her dark, brown eyes. Jo whispered a soft thank-you to her youngest daughter and thought that Jessica really had great patience for a sixteen-year-old. Years of sharing a room with a grandmother probably contributed to that.

As Grandma put on her seat belt, Jessica adjusted the mirror and began backing out of the long driveway. "Where do you need to go today, Grandma?" Jessica asked.

"Well, I need a little prune juice, and then I wanted to pick up a card for your daddy's birthday," was the reply. "You know, there was a time when I couldn't even afford a card for your daddy's birthday."

*Oh no,* thought Jessica, *not another story of how she raised six children with no husband around to help and how she worked in the school cafeteria to support them all.*

Jessica had heard these stories her whole life, and she really did sympathize with her, but did she have to hear them again today? Still she responded politely, "Yes, Grandma, I remember you telling me about those tough years. You really  have some great stories. But why don't we talk about *today?*"

Just then a car pulled out in front of Jessica. She slammed on her brakes, but there was no way she could stop soon enough. Jessica could hear the screeching of the tires and then the crunch of metal as the two cars collided.

Then she realized that even though she had hit the car, they were still moving. She reached up and put the car in park and it jolted to a stop. Jessica felt her head lunge forward, and her chin hit hard against the steering wheel.

"Jessica, are you okay?" Grandma Shack was yelling. Jessica felt something on her chin and realized it was blood, but she was okay.

"I'm fine, Grandma, what about you?"

"I think so. Just shaken up," she responded.

"Grandma, I can't open my door. I'm getting scared," Jessica cried.

"You're okay. I already hear a police car. Just hang on a minute." Grandma reassured her. Grandma was right. Jessica could hear a siren getting louder and louder.

"Grandma, I'm praying that God will help us get out of this wreck. And when we do, I promise I'll listen to any story you want to tell me about the old days."

The doctors and nurses were so nice at the emergency room. Jessica's teeth had gone through her chin as she hit the steering wheel, and that required several stitches. X-rays were taken and closely reviewed. Jessica and Grandma had pulled some muscles, but no bones were broken.

Friends and family poured into their house all that evening expressing concern and love. Grandma Shack and Jessica sat side by side, telling their story together. Jessica would begin with what road they were on and how scared she was when she looked up and saw the car pull out in front of them. Grandma would finish the story telling about Jessica's prayer and promise to listen to her stories. Everyone laughed as Grandma held Jessica's hand and told her she planned to hold her to that promise.

Later that night, after all the visitors left, Grandma and Jessica found that they were more than exhausted. They were also pretty sore. Jessica got her pajamas on and peeked into her old room where Grandma Shack had already climbed into the twin bed she had slept in for the last nine years. She looked over at this old woman who had shared her room for so many years. *Funny, what a difference a day makes!*

"Grandma, do you mind if I sleep in your room tonight?" Jessica asked.

"Of course not, Jessica. What's on your mind?" Grandma asked.

"I was just thinking how much I appreciate you and the sacrifices you made for your family. And how much you helped me today. Encouraging me to stay calm when I was really scared. There were probably lots of times when you were really scared and there was no one to help you. I just thought you might need me to sleep next to you tonight."

"I think that would be great," Grandma said. "I would love to have someone sleep near me tonight."

"Grandma, now that it's all over and we're okay," Jessica said in a sleepy voice, "I was just thinking how I can't wait to tell my grandchildren the story that we share together. It's a pretty good one, isn't it?"

*Record a story here that is worth passing on.*

_____

_____

_____

_____

_____

_____

_____

_____

_____

_____

_____

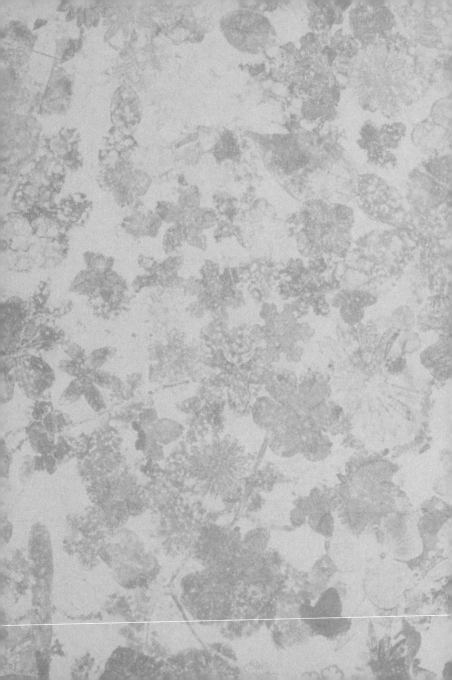

# You Are a
# Preserver of the Past

**6**

## Preserve It

$\mathcal{R}$emember the treasured traditions your ancestors have passed down to you. Reflect on your own cherished memories as you consider all the ways I've worked in your life. Share your sincere heritage of faith with your family for generations to come. Tell them of the days gone by and all My marvelous works. Your children and grandchildren applaud you and call you blessed.

Love,

*Your Rock of Ages*

—from Deuteronomy 32:7; 2 Timothy 1:5–6; Psalm 143:5; Proverbs 31:28

*Tradition!* Who can say that word without hearing the booming voice of Tevye from *Fiddler on the Roof*? Tevye was challenged with the dilemma of accepting new ways that seemed to interfere with what was traditionally accepted. What should he do? How could he mix the old with the new?

More importantly, what should you do, Grandma? You, like Tevye, have to be a defender and preserver of tradition! The minute you become a grandmother, it becomes your responsibility to polish all the family traditions and to prepare them for passage. Traditions are those important things that should be passed from one generation to another because tradition says that you are connected!

But we live in a very mobile society, and it isn't easy to keep traditions alive. Many would even argue against the value of tradition, stating that "times have changed." But no one will ever convince *you* that just because we have computers, a grandma with a good book has become obsolete or that a grandma's home cooking for Sunday lunch isn't the best meal in town just because we have restaurants on every corner. Just because families sometimes live clear across America from each other doesn't mean the highways won't continue to wear down from cars headed to Grandma's house every holiday. And just because we live in a time of "new" thinking doesn't mean that the "old" values of love, respect, honor, discipline, and dignity are out of date.

It's not that you don't like the new or don't welcome change. Who wants to go back to an icebox and candlelight? You love the new but want the best of the past to stay around awhile. And who can blame you?

So, Grandma, you keep on preserving and defending the traditions that make your family special. And never miss the opportunity to pass on something very important that was once passed on to you! If you ever stop, society will lose something very precious.

*You will find as you look back upon your life that the moments that stand out, the moments when you have really lived, are the moments you have done things in the spirit of love.*

—Henry Drummond

This year, Mama Sue had decided that
there would be no gingerbread house.

# The Gingerbread House

"Christmas Is for Kids," the song by the country group Alabama, played discreetly in the background. "Mama Sue," as her grandchildren called her, loved that song and believed it to be true. "Christmas *is* for kids," she sighed, exhausted from the long day of decorating. Mama Sue settled into her "grandma" chair for an evening of television and reading. Stockings that had weathered almost fifty Christmases hung once again over the fireplace, twinkle lights sparkled on a freshly cut tree, and colorful presents, carefully wrapped, completed the festive scene. Every house in Stillwater, Oklahoma, where she had lived for nearly seventy years, had a variety of stockings, lights, and presents.

Mama Sue knew that what had always set her house apart from the rest of Stillwater was her home-baked, meticulously decorated gingerbread houses. Red and green gumdrops lined the walls, white icing dripped from the roof, and candy canes carefully guarded the door. It was a child's dream house. One could almost picture a little elf peeking through the window, waiting for the night so he could come out and play. And when the gingerbread house was lov-ingly placed in the center of the dining room table, Christmas had officially arrived.

But this year, Mama Sue had decided that there would be no gingerbread house. Eventually all tradi-tions die, she had reasoned.

"Christmas is for kids," the chorus rang out once again. *But where are the kids?* she thought sadly. *I guess time marches on.* Her son and his family were almost two hours away. Her daughter lived in nearby Stillwater, but she was busy tonight with her own family projects.

## The Gingerbread House

Mama Sue knew they would all come over sometime during the holidays, but for the most part, the daily hustle and bustle of Christmas no longer affected her, and sometimes she missed it!

Some of it, of course, she didn't miss. The long lines at department stores. The kids' endless questions about Santa. The bills following the holiday season. But the kids, with rosy cheeks and sparkling eyes—those she missed. Especially Josh. There's something special, something unexplainable, something almost magical about that first grandchild. Maybe it's that just when you think you've reached a point in your life where maybe you're not so *needed*, you find yourself bound by the needs of a grandchild.

Josh certainly had fulfilled every grandmother's dream. Beautiful blue eyes, kind, gentle manners, strong and athletic, Josh was the first of eight beautiful grandchildren. She adored them all. But still, there's something special about the first.

The making of the gingerbread house began the year Josh was born. There's no denying that all the children loved it, but, for Josh, it truly was the symbol of Christmas. This would be Josh's first Christmas away from home. On December 22, he had married a beautiful girl from Louisiana. They had planned a two-day honeymoon to San Antonio and then Christmas would be spent with her family. Oklahoma was just too far to travel in that short amount of time. Of course, this was part of Mama Sue's decision not to make the gingerbread house. "I was there for the wedding, and it was great to spend time with him and to meet Ashley," she told herself. "He has better things to think about this Christmas than a silly old gingerbread house!"

As Mama Sue reached for the remote to see if *Touched by an Angel* had started, a soft voice seemed to say, "Where's the gingerbread house?" She tried to shake away the feeling as she flipped through the channels, but once again, from somewhere unknown, a little voice that sounded strangely like Josh's asked, "Where's the gingerbread house?"

"I'm tired," she announced out loud, as if to reaffirm to herself and the little voice that she truly was tired. After all, she hadn't fully recovered from that trip to Louisiana.

"Where's the gingerbread house?" the little voice nagged.

"That's it," she said. "What is this power grand-children have over us?" Putting down the remote and pushing down the footrest, Mama Sue declared, "It's not Christmas yet!"

With experienced hands and a grandmother's heart, the construction began. From walls to roof, this seemed to be the best house ever. As she placed the last gumdrop on the chimney, Mama Sue thought, *I wish I could see Josh's face when he opens the box.* But she could picture his face. She knew exactly what it would look like.

He would open the box, and a smile that could sell even bad toothpaste would light up his face. And, those eyes, as clear blue as the sky, would be almost closed as if his face could hold no more than the smile. What a gift he had been to her all these years! "I guess it's time for me to share Josh and my gingerbread house with others," she said. Off to the bedroom to find the sturdiest box she

had, Mama Sue now felt a sense of urgency. "This is going to have to go out by overnight express!"

It was the morning of Christmas Eve. Josh and Ashley were excited about their first Christmas together. The doorbell rang and Josh eagerly jumped up to see who had come to visit. After a few minutes, Josh declared, "Honey, it's Christmas!"

"I know," Ashley yelled back from the back room of their new house.

"No," said Josh, as he delicately placed the ginger-bread house on their dining room table, "I mean, it's officially Christmas!"

*Reflect on a special family tradition*
*that you have helped to preserve.*

_____

_____

_____

_____

_____

_____

_____

_____

_____

_____

_____

# You Are Hope

**7**

## Keep It Up

*H*ope in My good name! As you trust in Me, I'll fill you with all joy and peace, flooding your life with hope. Remember, your face reflects My glory. Even better, you're being transformed into My likeness with an ever-increasing glory. Surely My goodness and mercy will follow you and your family each and every day of your lives.

Making all things possible,
*Your God of All Hope*

—from Psalm 52:9; Romans 15:13;
2 Corinthians 3:18; Psalm 23:6; Matthew 19:26

*Grandmothers,* you are a model of hope to the young. *Hope* means to long for, to anticipate, to envision. Although you dreamed some dreams that never came true, set some goals that were never met, and had some ideas that never became reality, your grandchildren do not know that. They see dreams coming true when they attend a celebration honoring your many years of marriage. They see goals accomplished when someone hands you a gift in recognition of a job well done at a retirement party. They see your ideas become a reality when upon their graduation you present to them a quilt you've lovingly crafted.

You are the hope for a world of young people who are afraid to dream for fear their dreams won't come true. We look at a new baby and declare he or she is our hope for the future. And it's true. But hasn't the hope for tomorrow always depended upon the accomplishments of yesterday? The success and strength of America has always depended on the success and strength of our forefathers.

The same is true with your grandchildren. Their future depends in large part on your past. Your decisions, your dreams, your accomplishments are really the beginning of their lives. The most obvious decision affecting their very being was your choice of a life mate. Perhaps where they live now was also your decision many years ago. And perhaps even your job choices have affected your grandchildren. There are many families where "following in Grandma's footsteps" has produced teachers, nurses, or company presidents.

More important, you made a decision to live as a believer of Jesus, and now they have the chance to follow that path also. What a great connection! Just as God gives hope to a lost and dying world, you are a "hope-giver." Isn't it amazing to realize that many years after you are gone, you will live on! The strength of your past is the future of your grandchildren. And you're not through yet— keep up the good work!

*You are God's workmanship,*
*a quilt of beauty to behold.*

—Karla Dornacher

She had recently become a card-carrying
member of the "sandwich club."

# A Little Girl with a Grandma Face

Carol put the last of the dishes from lunch in the dishwasher, added the soap, and pushed the on button. *Whoever invented the dishwasher, thank you!* she thought. She had so much to do that day, and spending an hour washing dishes wouldn't have been one of her priorities. Defining her priorities these days had become rather difficult, as she had recently become a card-carrying member of the "sandwich club."

The *sandwich club* was the term used to refer to people who were caring for their aging parents as well as their own children. "Sandwiched between two generations" was the way the article had described Carol's stage of life. More than once in the last few years, Carol had scoured magazines for articles on caring for an aging parent, just as she had scoured magazines about pregnancy many years ago. She really couldn't believe how much information was available on the topic of aging. *Has there always been this much written about aging,* Carol wondered, *and I just didn't notice because it didn't affect me?* She couldn't help but wonder how many times she may not have noticed others who were facing the "sandwich" dilemma, never bothering to offer help or an encouraging word. *Well, now I know, and I promise to be more alert to others in the future.*

Carol had a bonus—maybe her situation was a "sandwich with the extras"—she now had grandchildren. Her oldest daughter was married with two

children, while her youngest daughter was a teenager still at home. Carol's priorities came from whoever needed her the most. On most days, she struggled with how to face toddlers, teens, and the elderly with equal enthusiasm. "I can do all things through Christ who strengthens me" was Carol's new favorite verse, and she quoted it often.

It wasn't as if she would change anything even if she could. When her mother began to have trouble functioning in her own house, Carol never questioned whether her mother would move in with her. And when her daughter needed help with her children, she always wanted to be there for her. And, of course, the demands of an active teenager with sports and school plays were ever present, and Carol was happy to be asked to help in whatever way she could. That's just the way she was raised. Family came first. But on some days, she was definitely ready for Calgon to "take her away."

Tossing the dirty dishtowel on the washing machine, she leaned over to pick up a roller skate that had made its way into the kitchen. The skate reminded her that she needed to check on the grandkids. They were in the living room playing with "Me-maw." Me-maw was the grandmother name all the kids called her mother. Entering the room, Carol found Me-maw on the floor playing with her great-grandchildren. Carol's daughter,

## You Are Hope—*Keep It Up*

Chrissy, had left her six-year-old daughter, Korie, and four-year-old son, Ryan, with her while she ran some errands. *If things were normal,* Carol thought, *I wouldn't have to look in on the kids while they played with Me-maw.*

But things were not normal and hadn't been for two years now. That's when the thief—as Carol called it—had entered her mother's home. That's when Me-maw was diagnosed with Alzheimer's disease. Carol had shared with her father that Alzheimer's was like a thief because it robbed her mother of so many things. Her command of language was gone, as well as her memory of all the years they had shared together. She now spoke in fragmented sentences and would forget events that happened just minutes before. And Carol knew that as time went on, her words and her memory would disappear entirely.

Carol had wanted her mother to stay in her own home in familiar surroundings as long as possible, but Carol had gradually begun to notice how difficult it was for her father to take care of her mother. When Carol would go over to check on them, she would find the cereal in the dishwasher and the milk in a cabinet. Finally, the time came to move them in with her.

Looking at her mom, playing peacefully with the children, Carol knew that if Alzheimer's hadn't come into Me-maw's life, she would have been up cooking and cleaning and listening to one of her favorite gospel music groups on the radio—singing along in her beautiful alto voice.

Carol was instantly grateful she had inherited her mother's voice and her blue eyes. *A constant reminder of what she once was*, Carol thought. But then Carol knew there were other reminders too: Me-maw's recipes she cooked for her own family and friends; phrases she said to her children; clothes she made using Me-maw's patterns; and quilts, casually thrown over beds and chairs, that had been pieced together by Me-maw's loving hands. Carol realized and was grateful that while the thief took her mother's memory, he had not taken hers. That's where Me-maw would live now and forever—in Carol's heart and mind.

And Carol would pass that memory on to her children and grandchildren.

*Everything changes when Alzheimer's enters your family. But life goes on, doesn't it?* Carol had half expected things to stand still as she cared for her mom, but she was so glad they hadn't. She knew that the seemingly small, insignificant, everyday events of life would help her get through the next few years. And seeing her grandchildren playing with Me-maw was one of those seemingly insignificant but extremely important events of this particular day. A memory had just been made. *Thank you, God, for this day and for this memory I'll always have of my mother.*

"Hey, Mom!" Chrissy said cheerfully as she walked into the living room, shaking Carol out of her thoughtful trance. "I got so much done today. Thanks for watching the kids. I don't know what I would do

 without you and Me-maw. Okay, kiddos, are you ready to go home?"

"Mom," said Korie, whose long curly hair had shaken free of the ponytail holder and now fell halfway down her back, "we've had the best time. We played

Barbies and drew pictures, and we went out back and picked up pecans. I think Me-maw's just like a little girl, only she has a grandma face!"

Tears came to Carol's eyes as she realized that her grandchildren were also forming memories. They weren't the same memories Carol had, but they were making their own. And as they grew older, Carol would be happy to add her memories of Me-maw to theirs.

*What strengths from your past are becoming*
*part of the future of your grandchildren?*

_____

_____

_____

_____

_____

_____

_____

_____

_____

_____

_____

Stories, Sayings, and Scriptures to Encourage and Inspire

# hugs

## for
## Granddaughters

CHRYS HOWARD
Personalized Scriptures by
LEANN WEISS

This book is dedicated to my
five precious granddaughters,

*Sadie, Macy, Ally,
Aslyn, and Bella.*

I love you more
than words can express
and enjoy every minute
I share with you!
May the Lord bless you
and keep you safe.

*Love, 2-Mama*

# Contents

Grandchildren are the
dots that connect
the lines from generation
to generation.

♦

Lois Wyse

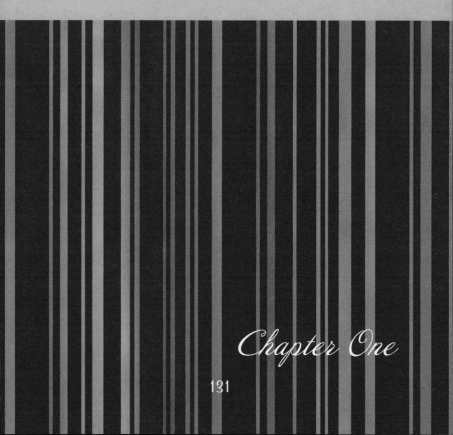

# Making Life Fun

## Chapter One

Enjoying life is a gift from Me to you. Let Me keep you occupied with a glad heart. Even before you were born, I thought countless precious thoughts of you and ordained all of your days. My love is always before you.

Smiling on you,
**Your God of Life**

—from Ecclesiastes 5:19–20; Psalms 139:16–17; 26:3

*When you were born,* your grandparents felt as though the world had stopped spinning. Busy schedules came to a sudden halt. Cameras flashed, tears flowed, and hands reached out to take their turn holding you. An actress making her debut on the red carpet wouldn't get more devoted attention than you did on your opening day! You were the center of their world.

Even today, the expression "wrapped around your little finger" doesn't begin to describe how important, how special, how much fun you are and always will be to your grandparents.

You see, somewhere along the way, before you came along, life had distracted them from the fun of picking a four-leaf clover or jumping into a swimming pool or riding a bike with no hands. But that's where a granddaughter comes in. You remind them how much fun life can be.

There's more to it than just the activities you share with them. Knowing how much you love them makes life more enjoyable. Your phone calls or e-mails are the best part of their day. And no matter how tired or how busy your grandparents are, they're always up for the special fun only a granddaughter can bring.

*What a grand thing
it is to be loved!
What a grander
thing it is to love!*

◆

Victor Hugo

Joanne had a hard time saying no to seeing her grandchildren, but the evening proved to be more of a challenge than she had anticipated.

# acts of love

Joanne rushed around the kitchen trying to get a hurried pot of meat sauce on the stove before her husband got home. She didn't always try to have supper on time—they had grown accustomed to eating out after work. But tonight she had so much to do at home that she had left work early and told her husband, Jim, that she might as well put something on for the two of them. After teaching school for many years, she loved the fact that her new schedule could be more flexible. Still, the bookkeeping responsibilities for their family-owned hardware store now rested heavily on her shoulders, and it seemed no matter how much she accomplished at the office, there was always more to do after working hours.

*I don't know if I should be thankful for computers or angry they were ever invented*, she thought as she looked at the laptop resting on the kitchen table, waiting for her to begin the night's work.

"Don't look at me like that!" Joanne warned the beckoning computer. "I have to finish supper, bake a cake, work on my Sunday-school lesson, clean the house, and wash a load of clothes before you even get opened." She smiled at herself for talking to a machine as she dumped a can of tomato sauce over the browned ground sausage.

The sudden musical tones from her cell phone startled her out of her harried concentration. She wiped her hands and fumbled through the clutter in her purse to retrieve the phone.

"Hello," she answered, trying not to sound like the interruption was unwelcome.

"Mimi?" said a faint little voice on the other end of the line.

"Sissy, is that you?" Joanne asked, knowing it was her seven-year-old granddaughter.

"It's me!" Sissy said, louder and more confident now that she knew she had dialed the right number.

"Hi, sweetheart, what are you doing?" Joanne asked, trying to hold the phone with her chin and shoulder while grabbing a cake mix from the pantry.

"Can I spend the night? Can I?" Sissy asked in her sweetest tone—the one that rarely received a negative reply.

But this was a night when Joanne was already overcommitted. Not wanting to turn her down directly, she decided to take another approach. "Sissy, Mimi has to bake a cake for Mrs. Potter, who is sick, and then take it to her house."

"I don't care," came the quick reply.

"Sissy, Mimi has to get the house cleaned and the clothes washed, because tomorrow night after work, I'm having company for dinner," Joanne tried again, wondering briefly why she always talked to her granddaughter in third person.

The sweet little voice came back undaunted. "I don't care."

Joanne offered one last excuse. "You know it's a school night, and you'll have to get in bed pretty early."

"I don't care."

She had met her match. Joanne smiled and at last gave in as she thought of Sissy's toothless grin and deep dimples. "Well, it's a date then. Go get Mommy and let me see if she'll bring you over."

"Hang on, I'll go get her!" Sissy said. Joanne imagined Sissy's brown ponytail bouncing with each step as she ran to find her mom.

As she'd been talking to Sissy, Joanne had poured the mix in to the bowl and added the water and three eggs. Now she started the mixer, knowing she couldn't spare one minute waiting for her daughter to come to the phone. Her mind was racing, knowing that having Sissy would add to her already busy evening. She didn't really mind. Sissy wasn't any trouble. She just wanted to be able to spend some quality time with her, and tonight's schedule didn't leave much room for that.

"Mom, can you hear me?" Joanne's daughter was yelling into the phone over the whirring of the mixer.

"Oh, I'm sorry, Melanie. I was mixing a cake while Sissy was getting you. I've got to get this in the oven for Sandy. She's just home from the hospital."

"That's okay. Mom, I didn't know Sissy was calling you. Now that she's memorized your cell-phone number, you'll have to tell her no sometimes. You know she'd sleep over there every night if we'd let her."

Joanne smiled at her daughter's warning.

"It's okay, Melanie, she's never any trouble. I just don't like it when I can't relax and enjoy being with her. I've got a pretty full schedule tonight, but she's welcome to come whenever you can bring her." Joanne licked off a bit of cake mix that had landed on her knuckle.

"Actually, I was about to leave the house to pick up some milk, so I'll bring her right over. Are you sure you don't mind?"

"Of course I don't mind. See you soon."

Joanne had made so many cakes in her life, she could do it blindfolded. It only took a few minutes to spray the pan, pour in the batter, and shut the oven door. *Now to the laundry,* she thought as she washed her hands. But again the phone rang.

"Hey, Momma." Joanne's youngest daughter was on the line.

"Hi, babe, did you have a good day?" Joanne asked, knowing Rebecca's day involved two toddlers, and the answer could easily be no.

"Pretty good. The kids actually took naps at the same time. Can you believe it?"

"Now that is a good day! I used to love it when you and your sister napped at the same time. I thought I was on vacation!"

"Mom, I know this is short notice," Rebecca said sheepishly, "but I need some help with the kids tonight."

"What's going on?" Joanne asked.

"Remember my friend, Amy? She had her baby today, and I really need to go see her. Her mom can't come until the weekend. I won't be gone long."

"I'm really busy tonight, but if you can deliver a cake to Sandy's house for me on your way back home, I guess I can watch them for a little while." Joanne had a hard time saying no to seeing any of her grand-children.

"Thanks, Mom. You're the best. I'll be there in about thirty minutes."

Joanne stirred the meat sauce one more time and went to collect the laundry. Hurrying back to the bathroom, she wondered where all that extra time was that she thought she'd have when the kids were grown. "Why can't Jim use a towel more than one time? My laundry duties would be cut in half if I could get that man to use a towel twice before throwing it on the floor. Oh well, you can't teach an old dog . . ." Joanne realized she was mumbling and shook her head as she gathered an armload of towels.

With the laundry started, Joanne returned to the kitchen. She opened the door of the refrigerator and then forgot why she had opened it.

Remembering it was the noodles she really wanted, she closed the refrigerator and headed for the pantry, thinking about an article she had read the night before about memory loss. *I should be cooking the foods mentioned in that article that would help my memory . . . if I could remember what they were,* she mused as she retrieved the pasta for her spaghetti supper.

"Mimi!" Sissy shrieked as she opened the back door. "I'm here!"

"Just in time to help me finish Papaw's supper. Have you eaten?" Joanne reached down for a big hug from her granddaughter.

"Not yet," Sissy said as she gave her grandmother a giant squeeze.

"Hi, Mom." Melanie greeted Joanne with the usual peck on the cheek. "Here's her suitcase. I'll have the carpool pick her up at your house. Call me if you get too busy and need me to come get her, okay?"

"We'll be fine," Joanne reassured her daughter. "Sylvan and Sara will be over in a minute while Rebecca goes to the hospital to see a friend. Sissy can help watch them."

"Oh, Mom, are you sure?" Melanie placed both hands on her hips for emphasis.

"Like I said, we'll be fine!"

But the evening proved to be more challenging than Joanne had anticipated. It didn't take her long to realize that spaghetti wasn't the best dinner for toddlers, and she wondered if the kids actually got any noodles inside their mouths. After the meal the babies were into everything, and Joanne felt as though she spent the whole time cleaning up messes instead of enjoying her little ones. Sissy proved to be a great help, but Joanne hated to keep asking her to entertain her cousins.

Two phone calls from friends at church and a stopped-up sink didn't help matters, and by the time Rebecca came to pick up the two toddlers and the hastily frosted cake, Joanne was exhausted. She still had to help Sissy go over her spelling words and take a bath. She was thankful that at least her granddaughter's memory was still intact, and they were able to get through the words fairly quickly.

"Sissy, I'll run your bathwater while you go get your suitcase," Joanne said, yawning and rubbing her aching back.

"JOANNE . . . telephone!" Her husband called out over the sound of running water. "It's your mother."

Joanne knew this would be a long phone call, so she told Sissy to go ahead and bathe herself. Even though, at seven years old, Sissy was fully capable of doing that and washing her own hair, Joanne felt a twinge of guilt at not being able to help her. She reached over and pulled Sissy close to her. "I am so proud of you for being able to take care of yourself and for helping me with your cousins. After your bath, I'll read you a story," she promised.

The phone call took longer than Joanne expected, though, and soon she looked up to see a squeaky clean, wet-headed Sissy sitting beside her. She was already in her pajamas, so Joanne whispered that she needed to go ahead and get in bed and that she would be in soon. Sissy looked disappointed but shuffled off to the bedroom she always slept in.

When Joanne finished the conversation with her mother, she hurried off to check on Sissy. Her heart sank a little when she found Sissy already fast asleep, her angelic face surrounded by wet curls. She gathered up her wet hair so it wouldn't rest on her shoulders, straightened the blanket, and gave her a kiss.

"I'm sorry, sweetheart," she whispered in her granddaughter's ear. "We'll read a book next time."

Too tired to tackle the bookkeeping or the Sunday-school material, Joanne finished putting the dishes in the dishwasher and decided that now was a good time for her to soak in the tub. She turned the dimmer switch down in the bathroom and lit an aromatherapy candle.

"Boy, do I need this," she said aloud, feeling the warm water graze her fingertips as she brought it to a good bath temperature.

Her large sunken bathtub was used more often as a mini-swimming pool by her grandchildren than as a comfort station for herself, but tonight it was her turn. She was feeling every bit of being a grand-mother. Sylvan was a big two-year-old, and every time he came to visit, Joanne ended up feeling like she needed a trip to the chiropractor. She wiped up the sloshed water from Sissy's bath and gathered a clean towel and washcloth for herself.

She stepped into the tub and, with her eyes closed, settled down into the warmth that immediately relaxed her tired body. *Poor Sissy*, she thought. *All she wanted was a little attention.* She remembered her granddaughter's dejected expression. *I wish I could soak that away.* Joanne sighed and opened her eyes.

Through the steam, something red, blue, and yellow caught her attention. *Probably some leftover toys from the kids.* As she leaned forward, there on the side of the tub, just above the water level and written with colored-gel bath soaps, was a message: "I love you, Mimi."

Joanne could barely swallow the lump in her throat as she thought of the little girl lovingly and determinedly finding a way to connect with her grandmother. She smiled as a tear slipped down her cheek. No aromatherapy could match this. However hectic things got, nothing could interrupt the love between a grandmother and her granddaughter.

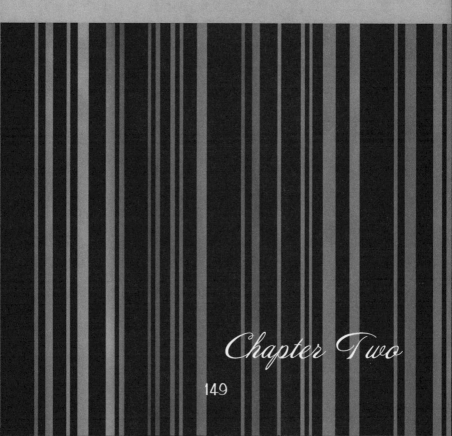

# Understanding the Past

*Chapter Two*

Celebrate your differences. You are My treasured masterpiece. You can be confident that I'll always complete the unique work I've started in you.

Creatively,
Your Forever Faithful God

—from Romans 12:6; Ephesians 2:10; Philippians 1:6

*Sometimes it's hard* to understand the past—to see how it connects to the present and links inevitably to the future. But it does.

You, granddaughter, are the one who will carry on the traditions established by your grandparents and reinforced by your parents. You're an invaluable link in the family chain. You've heard stories and seen pictures that have the power to bring the stability of the past to the confusion of the present and the uncertainty of the future.

Your family is depending on you to hang on to those traditions. They're part of what identifies you as a family and gives you a distinctive bond. Perhaps you had an Indian grandmother who still wore a sari on special occasions, or a grandfather who remembered the old Irish songs and sang them with a thick brogue. Maybe your grandmother always baked a coconut cake at Easter. Whatever the traditions, you know the stories behind them. And you strive to keep the family spirit alive—for yourself, your children, and eventually your grandchildren.

Few things are more important to our future than our past—especially how we use the lessons we've learned to impact the world around us.

Granddaughter, as you preserve the parts of your past, the memories flavored with meaning, may they add as much richness to your life as you add to the lives of those around you.

*You are here
to enrich the world,
and you impoverish
yourself if you forget
the errand.*

◆

**Woodrow Wilson**

"You look so beautiful," Jennifer's grandmother gushed. But Jennifer wrinkled her nose in disgust.

# the art of being different

"Mom, it just doesn't matter," fourteen-year-old Jennifer Maddox yelled from the top of the staircase, straining to keep her voice within the limits she knew her mother would allow without dealing out punishment.

"It matters to me." Jennifer heard the exasperation in her mother's voice but chose to ignore it. She knew her mother was downstairs gathering up the last-minute items needed for the party, but Jennifer's mind was solely on her clothes.

"But you're the only one who cares! Nana never cares what I wear. Pleeeease!" Her plea seemed to fall on deaf ears. Her mother didn't even acknowledge her words.

Stomping back into her room, Jennifer grabbed the dress her mother had picked out for her and kicked off the army boots she had wanted to wear. "Why did I have to be born into this family," she grumbled to herself. "What a boring mother—she's never any fun!"

Her scowl faded a little as she caught a glimpse of herself in the mirror and paused to admire her reflection. Her new hairstyle with its short, bleached-and-spiked tips was perfect for her small face. She couldn't believe her uptight mother had agreed to let her get such a cool cut. Then she touched her newly pierced left ear. *I can't wait to show Nana*, she thought as she relished her success last Saturday: talking her mom into letting her have not just one but two holes in her left ear. *Now I'm getting somewhere*, she had thought. Today she was a little more cynical. *Mom must have been in a really good mood that day—unlike today, when she insists on my wearing this stupid dress!*

Somewhere in the back of Jennifer's mind, she knew she loved her mother very much. But they were so different. Jennifer's casual, slightly edgy attitude clashed with her mother's more reserved worldview. To say they approached life from different angles was an understatement, and tonight's showdown had been just one more in an endless series over the years.

"Jen, please hurry. Your grandma's party starts at seven, and I'm in charge of greeting the guests."

Jennifer took in a deep breath and rolled her eyes. *She's always in charge of something.* She reached over her head to finish zipping up her dress. *I wish she could just chill out for one day.*

"Time to go," her mom shouted from the end of the staircase. "I'll be in the car."

Jennifer took one more look in the mirror and muttered to herself. "What's so wrong with wanting to wear jeans instead of a dress? She thinks everyone should be just like she is. Doesn't she understand that I'm a person too?"

She spiked her hair a little higher, then stomped out of her bedroom. She made sure the door slammed behind her, knowing there was no one in the house to hear the sound of protest, but still feeling better for having done it.

The drive to her grandma's seventieth birthday party was silent except for the overflow of blaring music she defiantly made sure could be heard from her headset. She didn't want to risk a conversation with her mother. She bobbed her head up and down and back and forth to the beat and, for a moment, lost herself in the music.

"Jennifer, could you please turn the volume down. I can't hear myself think, and I'm not even wearing the earphones! You're going to lose your hearing one day." Jennifer rolled her eyes again and turned the volume down one level.

They arrived at the restaurant before any of the guests, but Jennifer's grandma, Judy, was already sitting in the reception area waiting for them. Jennifer loved her grandmother immensely. They shared a unique bond because they were both artists. Her grandma loved to paint and had introduced Jennifer to the world of color and design at an early age. To her grandmother's delight, Jennifer had taken to art naturally and showed promising talent. Together they had created many masterpieces, most decorating the retired woman's refrigerator—but masterpieces just the same.

Jennifer greeted her grandmother with a big hug. "Nana, what do you think of my haircut?"

Judy held Jennifer by the shoulders at arm's length to get a good look. "Why, I think it looks just like you," she answered diplomatically. "You always look beautiful to me. And what's that I see in your ear?"

"Isn't it cool? Mom let me do it last weekend. Everyone's getting their ears pierced multiple times."

Now Jennifer's mother rolled her eyes. "You always say to pick your battles," she said with a resigned smile. "Happy birthday, Mom." She gave her mother a hug.

"Thank you, sweetheart. It's wonderful of you and your brother to do this for me. I hope you didn't go to too much trouble."

"Nonsense! You couldn't turn seventy without a party. We've been looking forward to this evening. If you'll excuse me for just a minute, I need to check with the manager to make sure everything's ready. Call me picky, but I just can't leave anything to chance. I'll be right back."

"Jennifer, you look so beautiful," Jennifer's grandmother gushed as she motioned for her granddaughter to sit beside her.

Jennifer wrinkled her nose in disgust. "Mom made me wear this dress. I had picked out the coolest black shirt and jeans to wear. And I have a new belt that hangs really low on my hips. But you know Mom, she said I had to look 'nice.' I thought it *did* look nice."

"Yes, I know your mom. I raised her." She chuckled. "And on some days, that was quite a challenge."

"It was?" Jennifer's eyes widened as she waited for the inside scoop on her "perfect" mother.

"You bet. We're just so different. No matter how hard I pushed, she hated art classes. And to be honest, she was never very good—couldn't draw a stick figure. You know, Jennifer, God has given you a gift in your artistic ability. I've seen it from the time you were two years old."

Jennifer could already feel her spirits rise. Her grandmother always had a way of making her feel good about herself.

"Did you and Mom fight about everything?" she pleaded, wanting more details.

"Well, not everything. You know, it's important to remember that God has made each of us uniquely special. Your mother has many talents I don't have—like organizing and taking charge of things. Sure, I would have liked it if she had been artistic, but what I really wanted was for her to be herself. It's the same with you and your mom—you both have wonderful qualities, they're just different. And that means the things you like to do or the clothes you choose to wear may not be what she would choose."

"Tell me about it," Jennifer mumbled and hung her head.

Her grandmother lifted Jennifer's face and looked her in the eye. "But Jennifer, don't ever doubt that your mother wants the same for you that I wanted for her—to be your best self. There will be times when you don't agree on things, but those little differences are just about style and individual taste. They have nothing to do with your mother's love for you and her pride in you. Those are unchanging."

Jennifer's shoulders remained slumped. "I know you're probably right, but why doesn't she like anything I like, when you like everything I like?"

Her grandmother smiled sagely. "You have to remember, your mom is the one in the responsible position, while I get to just join in for the fun! When I was raising your mom, I was the one who had to be responsible. That's a much tougher job.

"Speaking of fun . . ." Jennifer's grandmother reached down and pulled a little package from her purse. "I brought you something."

"Nana, I'm the one who's supposed to bring *you* a gift. It's your birthday!" Jennifer laughed with glee at the surprise.

"It's my birthday, and I can give a gift if I want to. After all, it is more fun to give than to receive." She handed Jennifer a tiny box wrapped in pink paper and tied with a black bow.

"I love pink and black! You're the coolest grandmother ever." Jennifer opened the package and was thrilled to find a new set of pierced earrings—and one extra earring.

"Oh, Nana, they're perfect. I can't wait until I can take out these studs and wear these new earrings. But how did you know I had gotten my ears pierced? I just told you tonight."

Her grandmother smiled and replied with a wink. "Your mother called me and told me how excited you were and how cute you looked. She's really not such a bad mom after all, now is she?"

Jennifer looked down at the earrings and then at her grandmother. "I guess you're right." Her lips curled up in a smile. "But I'm still glad you're around to have fun with!"

"Me too," her grandmother said. "Now let's go to a party!"

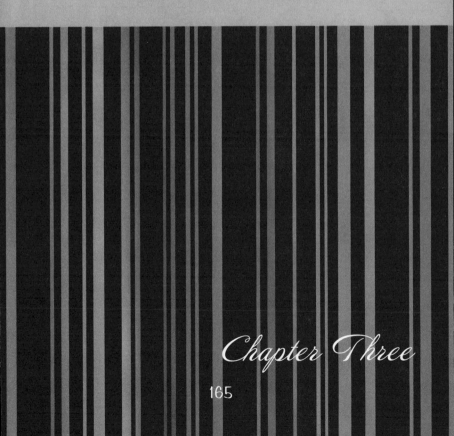

# Staying Connected

## Chapter Three

165

Call upon Me and I'll answer you. Find comfort in My ancient ways. My unfailing love is your solace. No matter what, I'm committed to you! I'm always watching over your life.

Loving you always,
Your God of All Comfort

—from Jeremiah 33:3; Psalm 119:52, 76;
Deuteronomy 31:6; Psalm 121:8; 2 Corinthians 1:3

*In the hustle and bustle* of your day, amid all the exciting challenges in your life, you probably sometimes feel you don't have the time to keep up with family—to make that phone call or write that letter. But you do it anyway, because as a granddaughter you know the importance of staying connected to the people who love you and whom you love.

It's said that no man is an island, and you know that's true. As you navigate through life with its twists and turns, you and your grandparents have been there for one another. Whether it's their cheers at a ball game or their birthday cards with ten-dollar bills in them, your holiday visits or your phone calls just to say hi, you share a special bond with them because you are a special grand-daughter.

Staying connected is easier today than when your grandparents were children, but it still takes time, effort, and care. Maybe even more so because we're all moving so fast it's hard to slow down and take time for relationships. But when we do, we weave a rich tapestry of love. That's a lesson you learned from your grandparents, and it's a blessing you give back to them every time you call, write, or e-mail just to say I love you.

Sure, times have changed. But with wonderful granddaughters like you, staying connected remains a time-less treasure.

*If I can put one touch
of rosy sunset into
the life of any man or
woman, I shall feel
that I have
worked with God.*

◆

George MacDonald

Missy put her head in her hands, feeling close to tears. "Working in New York is something I've always wanted to do. Why am I feeling so torn all of a sudden?"

# the comfort quilt

Missy meandered through her grandmother's house, acutely aware of her surroundings. Rubbing her fingers along the antique dining room table, she thought of the many meals she had eaten there. Even now her grandmother was in the kitchen preparing a special dinner for her. The humming she heard over the chopping and dicing was her grandma's favorite hymn. The scent, overpowering even the cinnamon potpourri synonymous with her grandmother's inviting home, was from Missy's favorite dish, roast beef. She stopped for a moment to savor the aroma, her mouth watering in anticipation.

*And He walks with me and He talks with me.* Silently, Missy filled in the words to the tune coming from the kitchen. *Mamaw has taught me so much,* she thought as she continued her farewell tour through the house. She looked over the dining room table, past the antique furniture and accents perfectly arranged to break up the long space across the front of the house, to the far side of the living room. *I'll bet I could make it to the couch blindfolded.*

For twenty-four years she had been a part of this house. She had played dominoes and checkers on every tabletop, hide-and-seek in every closet and under every bed. She'd dressed up dolls and pushed them in their miniature strollers from one room to the next. Missy closed her eyes. This was as good a time as any to try her walk of faith. She set off toward the couch. Within seconds she had reached the sofa unhindered and sat down, snuggling a pillow to her chest and breathing in the clean, familiar smell.

*Hours on this couch*, she thought. Scenes of late-night talks with her grandmother ran through her mind: When she was six, she had asked her grandmother what happens when pets die. As a teenager she had cried to her about awful dates. She'd done countless homework assignments stretched out here. More recently she had announced with excitement— and a little fear—the job offer in New York City. How encouraging and assuring her grandmother had been.

*Why am I feeling so torn all of a sudden? Working in New York is something I've always wanted to do. I can't back out now*. Missy put her head in her hands, feeling close to tears.

"Missy," her grandmother called out. "Would you set the table for me? I'm running a little behind."

Missy took a deep breath and straightened her back, forcing herself back into composure. "Sure, give me a minute. I'm just checking on a few things."

She stood up and started back toward the dining room but couldn't help pausing when she caught sight of the quilt rack. Her grandmother always had a handmade quilt hanging there, waiting to be given to someone who needed special care. Her family had dubbed them comfort quilts. Growing up, Missy had watched her grandmother quilt her way through every triumph and tragedy. She quilted for the birth of new babies, and she quilted for friends who were hospital bound. Missy couldn't help but walk over and finger the edges. The needlework seemed to represent everything her grandmother stood for: courage, hospitality, resourcefulness, caring. For some reason, tonight the quilt felt almost magical. Missy had never really paid much attention to the pattern or the choice of fabrics. But tonight she noticed. The varying shades of blue had been stitched together masterfully, each shade complementing the others.

*Wow, this one is really beautiful. I love blue. I can't believe I never had Mamaw teach me to quilt.* She sighed deeply, feeling suddenly remorseful at the lost opportunity, then joined her grandmother in the kitchen.

"What was that?" her grandmother asked.

"Oh, nothing, Mamaw. Everything smells wonderful!" She gave her grandmother a kiss on the cheek. "Thank you for doing this for me. I'm going to miss this so much!"

"It's a labor of love." Her grandmother returned the kiss. "And don't go acting like you won't be back. Any time you're in town, this kitchen will be open for service. Right now we had better hurry. Your parents will be here in fifteen minutes, and we're not quite ready. You know how your daddy hates to wait!"

Missy smiled as she thought of her dad coming in, removing the lid from the roast, and saying, "Smells good, when do we eat?"

"Let's use the good china tonight," her grandmother suggested. "You know where everything is."

Missy went to the dining room and carefully lifted the plates from the china cabinet. Once her grandma had explained how Grampa had surprised her with the china on their fifteenth wedding anniversary. He had shopped and shopped, looking for the perfect pattern to surprise his wife. As Missy peered at her reflection in the cream-colored plates with their gold rims, she thought her grandpa had done a great job. *It must not look a day older than it did when Grandma opened the original box.* She raised an eyebrow. *Of course, it's not like it should be worn out from overuse. I'll bet I could count on my fingers how many times I've seen these plates out. Special occasions, that's it.* Suddenly it sunk in that this time *she* was the special occasion.

"Oh, Missy," her grandma called from the kitchen. "Can you also set out the silverware? A few spoons are missing, but there should be enough."

Missy grinned. She knew the missing spoons were probably her doing back when she was a child holding pretend tea parties.

Just then she heard the front door open and a loud "Mmm-mm. Something sure smells good! When do we eat?"

Missy shook her head and laughed. *There's Dad.*

"How about a hug and then I'll think about putting food on the table?" she heard her grandma say. "First things first!"

"That's what I was talking about. First things first. Where's the food?"

Missy hung back, listening to the familiar banter. *That, I will miss. It's hard to capture that in a letter or an e-mail.*

"Hey, Mom and Dad." Missy went to the kitchen and hugged each of her parents.

"What do I need to do?" her mom asked as she washed her hands, preparing to help.

Missy's grandmother directed her answer at her son, who was picking at the roast with a fork. "We're just waiting on the rolls."

"All right, all right. Can I help it if I think you're a fabulous cook? Do you want me to carve the roast?"

"Yes, if you think you can keep from eating the whole thing in the process!"

Soon the roast was on the table, the rolls were buttered, and the family was seated and talking animatedly about the adventures of their week. Missy soaked in every detail, relishing the laughter and love that filled the room. Finally, she cleared her throat. "Can I have your attention please?" She swallowed hard, not wanting to cry just yet.

"I know I'm not leaving for a few days, but I've been thinking about what it means to be part of a family that loves and supports you. And I've concluded it means everything. Tonight I got here early because I wanted some quiet time alone in this house, touching, smelling, and remembering everything I've done here.

"There's something extraordinary about a grandparent's house that I can't quite explain. It's like your own house because you feel like everything is yours, yet you're treated like a special guest. I want to thank you, Mamaw, for the heritage of a family whose greatest tradition is to love one another. It all started with you and Grandpa. You two passed it on to Daddy, and he and Mom have taught me. I just want you all to know that no matter where I am, you are the most important people in the world to me, and I love you."

Missy's mother picked up a napkin and dabbed away a tear. Her dad pretended to be clearing his throat. Missy's grandmother was the first to speak, her voice thick with emotion. "Well, if I can manage it, I have something special to share too." The room got even quieter as she got up and walked over to stand behind Missy.

Missy closed her eyes, sure she couldn't hold back tears much longer.

"You all know how much I love this little girl." Her grandmother patted Missy on the shoulder as if she were still five years old. "I know she's all grown up, but she's still my little Missy. Her decision to move to New York is a brave one, and I want her to know how proud I am of her adventurous spirit and her desire to make her own way. But she's right— family is the most precious gift we have. So I have something for you—for the days when you're missing that family connection and you need someone to

wrap loving arms around you and hold you tight."
She made her way over to the quilt rack.

Missy held her breath as her grandmother picked
up the quilt and began unfolding it with as much care
and ceremony as a marine unfolding the American
flag. As she exposed each layer, the hours of work
it had obviously taken, the tiny stitches that formed
an intricate design, were evidence of how she loved
Missy.

Missy rose and wrapped her arms around her
grandmother, quilt and all. "Oh, Mamaw, this is for
me? It's the best gift ever!"

"Wait," her grandmother said with a gleam in her
eye. "You haven't seen the best part."

Missy helped her grandmother unfold the quilt
the rest of the way. When it was open, her grandmother instructed her to turn it over and look at the
other side.

Missy gasped. She couldn't believe her eyes. Right
in the middle of the quilt was a collage of pictures
that had been scanned onto the individual squares
of fabric—Missy and her parents and grandparents
at various stages of their lives. Now the tears were
unstoppable, and Missy grabbed her grandmother
again in a tight embrace. Their special bond had been
captured forever in the most beautiful quilt she had
ever seen. Now, no matter where she was, all she had
to do to feel at home was touch the comfort quilt.

# Feeling Loved

*Chapter Four*

181

*You can't begin to measure My love for you. It's even better than life. I keep My covenant of love to a thousand generations. You can count on My goodness and love every day.*

Eternal hugs,
## Your God of Love

—from Psalms 103:11; 63:3; Deuteronomy 7:9; Psalm 23:6

*Isn't it fun* to be the center of attention? Whether it's your kindergarten graduation or your wedding day, you are *it*! All the cameras and lights are on you.

But special occasions only come along once in a while. Want to enjoy that special place of importance every day? You don't have to climb Mount Everest or win a beauty contest. You don't have to prove or earn anything. You are a granddaughter.

The moment you came into this world, you changed your grandparents' lives forever— just by being you. You give them someone to love, someone to shower attention on and to delight in.

And the best thing is it doesn't have to be a special day, like a graduation or a wedding, for you to be the most important person in the world to them. It can just be any day and anytime—it's every day and all the time.

You are reason enough for celebration—no special occasion needed. It doesn't matter what you look like or how talented you are or what anyone else thinks of you. Your grandparents think you're perfect just the way you are. Their hearts were given to you on an unconditional silver platter the minute you were born. No matter what else happens, you, granddaughter, hold an irrevocable place of importance in their hearts.

*To us, family means
putting your arms
around each other
and being there.*

◆

Barbara Bush

Everything was in place
for the wedding
of her dreams.
There had been no
snags . . . until now.

# in sickness and in health

Shelly looked at her fresh set of French-manicured, sculpted nails. *If they weren't so lovely, I'd bite them right off.* She was so nervous that her old nail-biting habit had returned with a vengeance. But her grandmother had treated her and her bridesmaids to manicures the day before, and now as she placed her hands delicately on the white skirt of her wedding gown, her thoughts again returned to her grandma.

*This can't be happening.* She sighed and started pacing the floor of the tiny bride's room.

There had been no snags until now. The flowers were the exact color she wanted. The bridesmaids' dresses fit perfectly. The rehearsal had gone smoothly. Everything was in place for the wedding of her dreams, and she knew the credit went to her grandmother, who had poured countless hours of love and energy into making this day as wonderful as even a princess could have wished.

Shelly's grandmother had been a much sought-after wedding planner. Mothers had loved her attention to detail, and fathers her ability to work magic with any wedding budget. When she retired ten years earlier, she had promised Shelly she would come out of retirement to plan her only granddaughter's wedding. Since Shelly was a girl, they had poured over bride magazines together, picking out the perfect flowers and designing and redesigning wedding cakes—all in anticipation of the day Shelly would walk down the aisle in a fairy-tale setting created by her grandmother.

But just a few hours ago, Shelly's mother had tapped her gently on the shoulder. "Shelly, I don't want you to panic. Everything is okay. I just have to tell you something."

Speechless, Shelly had just stared at her mother. Surely those words on your wedding day would seem the perfect time to panic. The possibilities were swirling in her imagination: the cake falling on its way to the church, the church catching fire from a stray candle, the photographer not showing up . . .

"Don't panic!" She remembered her voice catching somewhere in her throat before squeaking out. "What does that mean? What happened?" She had tried to stay calm, but a sickening feeling had taken hold of her stomach almost instantly.

"Your grandpa just called, and Grandma is at the hospital. She wasn't feeling well when she woke up this morning, but she just kept going to make sure everything was ready for tonight."

Shelly's eyes widened as she listened to the details, now focused on her grandmother's health and not yet considering the impact the news would have on her own plans. Her mother continued. "She was talking to the florist one last time when nausea overcame her, and she became very sick."

"She'll be okay by the wedding, won't she?" The expression in her voice was seeking confirmation rather than an answer to a question.

"Well, honey," Shelly's mom responded guardedly, "Grandpa said he took her on to the hospital hoping they could give her something to get her through the wedding, but he said he wasn't sure it would work."

Somewhere in the middle of her concern for her grandmother's health, it hit her. The candles were only minutes away from being lit, the finishing touches of pink roses were being added to the three-tier cake—and her wedding planner was in the hospital.

"Oh, Mom." Shelly bit her lip. "She's the one who knows everything. When the music starts, who wears a corsage, when the candle lighters start—"

"We'll be just fine," Shelly's mom said reassuringly. "We practiced last night, and everyone knows what to do. Besides, I've heard your grandmother say many times, 'You can't mess up a wedding.'"

Shelly could hear her grandmother's voice in those words, and she relaxed a little, but she still didn't like the thought of her strong, always proper grandma on a gurney in the emergency room. The matriarch of their family stood five feet ten inches tall, with piercing blue eyes and Clairol-brown hair. No one ever suspected she was seventy-five years old. She was a tower of strength to Shelly—someone she called whenever she needed sound, no-nonsense advice.

"Mom, remember last night when Grandma insisted on bringing a fruit tray to have here for the bridesmaids to munch on? I'll bet she's thinking about that right now. She wanted everything to be so perfect."

"I'm sure you're right." Her mom shook her head and smiled. "She's probably still trying to figure out how she can get a fruit tray up here. Grandpa said to tell you she whispered between waves of nausea, 'Tell Shelly not to worry. At six o'clock, I'll be there!'"

Shelly's lip quivered as she thought of her sweet grandmother, with whom she had shared so many of her wedding dreams, not being able to see it all come true. She closed her eyes and said a prayer for her grandmother's health.

"Mom, should we postpone the wedding for an hour or so? Grandma would be so sad if she missed it. What should we do?"

"Sweetie, it's too late to change the schedule now. The music will start at six o'clock, and you will walk down the aisle just as you and your grandmother planned." Shelly's mom reached over and grabbed her worried daughter's hand. "She had everything organized; the wedding will go smoothly and be lovely. Your grandmother will be sad if she misses it, but she would be beside herself if she knew you were even thinking of delaying it because of her. Grandpa said she'll be fine and for us to not worry. Now let's get downstairs for pictures."

Shelly hoped and prayed that her smile didn't look too fixed in the photo session as she tried to remain calm and not focus too much on her grandma's illness. She had made her mother promise to keep her updated if any news came in.

The last call her mother received was at four o'clock, and Shelly's grandmother was being released but was still very sick. "Dad, tell her to go straight home and rest. The wedding will be videotaped, and she can watch it later," Shelly responded.

*Feeling Loved*

Shelly was listening to her mother talk and wanted to agree with her, yet she couldn't help wishing her grandmother would come to the wedding. After all the years of planning, it was almost unthinkable to go through it without her.

Shelly looked at her watch. Five-fifteen. *She's not going to make it. How can I get married without Grandma?*

Just then the door opened and her mother appeared. "They want us to start lining up. Are you ready?"

Shelly knew her mom was doing her best to be cheerful and positive and to ensure that her special day wasn't ruined.

"Sure, Mom," Shelly said, blinking back a tear.

"Let me have one last hug before I have to share you forever with the man of your dreams." Her mom held her extra tight as she whispered, "Here's a hug from your grandmother. She'll love the pictures. You look beautiful!"

"Thank you, Momma." Shelly sniffled and took a deep breath. "I'm ready. I guess that old saying is true: 'The best laid plans of mice and men often go awry.' I sure didn't expect Grandma to miss this wedding, but I know it'll be okay."

"That's my girl! You know, your grandmother

would say wild horses couldn't keep her from being at your wedding. You know she'd be here if she could."

Shelly's mom walked behind her to hold the long, beaded train in the air as Shelly walked down the hall and into the foyer of the church building. Shelly clung to her flowers and nervously played with her engagement ring as she practiced the timing of her steps, mentally humming the wedding march.

Her dad greeted her at the back of the chapel. "Where did my little girl go?" he asked as he kissed her cheek. "I haven't seen such a beautiful bride since your mother took my breath away twenty-five years ago." Seeing her stoic father tear up surprised her and tore at her heart.

"Oh, Daddy—" She returned her dad's kiss and smiled as she wiped the faint lipstick smudge off his cheek. "I love you so much."

The bridesmaids were taking their slow walk toward the stained-glass front of the chapel. Shelly could see that the little sanctuary was almost full with her family and friends. Everything was perfect. *Grandma would have loved this.*

Suddenly the music changed, and she felt her father's nudge to move up to the archway where their walk would begin. She caught her breath as she saw everyone stand and face her. This was it—the moment she had dreamed of.

Shelly smiled as her dad patted her arm. She felt almost as if she were gliding down the aisle on a magic carpet, her gaze meeting that of her husband-to-be. Then, as if by impulse, she looked toward the pew where her grandparents were to be seated—and discovered, to her surprise, that they were right where they were supposed to be, smiling and crying!

She couldn't make herself keep walking. She had to stop and hug her grandma. "Grandma, what are you doing? I thought you were going home after they released you!"

"I promised you I'd be here at six o'clock. Wild horses couldn't have kept me from sharing this day with you!"

Shelly laughed and took her place again beside her dad. As she started back down the aisle, she mouthed "I love you" to her grandmother. She didn't have to wait for her grandmother to mouth it back. She already knew.

# Being
# Supportive

*Chapter Five*

*Even before you ask, I know your needs. I am able to provide all of your needs according to My unlimited riches in glory. You can wait in hope for Me because I'm your help and your protection.*

Supporting you,
## Your Heavenly Father

—from Matthew 6:8; Philippians 4:19; Psalm 33:20

*Only a handful of people* know almost everything about you. It's a small minority that knows whether you eat spinach or like scary movies. Your parents, maybe your best friend . . . and your grandparents. Having people around who know you so well that they can sense a need and act on it is one of the best feelings in the world, and that's just the kind of feeling a grandparent-granddaughter relationship can bring.

Yet you've never allowed yourself to stay only on the receiving end of your grandparents' affection. You give your amazing love and support to them as well. And through the years, they've come to know they can depend on you.

Your love for them and your concern for their well-being is evident and invaluable. While they would do anything for you, what's even more special is knowing you would do anything for them.

That's what a support system is. It sustains you through good times and bad. Whether it's late at night or early in the morning, you're there for each other.

Today's society is mobile, and grandparents may be more active for longer than ever before—traveling, taking classes, or launching second careers. But they still need you and want to be part of your life. A loving, supportive relationship with you, their granddaughter, is a joy and a blessing.

*The smallest seed
of faith is better than
the largest fruit
of happiness.*

◆

Henry David Thoreau

Anne chased her giggling, diaper-trailing toddler down the hall. "What am I doing wrong?" she lamented.

# the dinner guest

Anne was up to her ears in poop. Well, almost. She had a baby in diapers, a toddler being potty trained, and two cats that had suddenly developed an aversion to their litter pan. Sometimes she felt as though her entire day revolved around cleaning something up.

Today had been no different, and she was exhausted. But finally, for a few precious minutes, the house was relatively quiet. Two-year-old Jesse was entertaining himself in his room; baby Gracie was sitting quietly on Anne's lap, and the cats had been put out to wander in the yard. Anne wouldn't have been too disappointed if they wandered away entirely.

She had just picked up a novel she was determined to read when the phone rang. Anne sighed. She was tired of all the telemarketing calls and was sorely tempted to ignore it—to launch her own personal phone strike. But she put the book down, hiked Gracie on one hip, and picked up the receiver. *Maybe it's Calgon calling to take me away,* she thought wryly.

"Hi, Anne, this is Granny. How are you?"

"Oh, Granny. Hi! I'm fine. How are you?" It was almost as good as Calgon. Anne loved the sound of her grandmother's voice. It was so soothing and always sincere.

"Well, honey, I'm doing pretty well. I just wanted to see how my babies were."

"They're great too. But Granny, I think I started this whole process too late. You had your babies young, when you had lots of energy. I thought after running an office, motherhood would be easy. I had no idea how hard this could be."

Granny Grace laughed. "I seem to recall someone who said having babies in her thirties would mean she'd be more mature and able to handle it." Even when she was teasing, Anne could hear the sympathy in her grandmother's voice.

"Did I say that? What was I thinking?" Anne laughed too, knowing it was the truth. "Although I seem to recall someone saying, 'You're probably right!'"

Granny Grace sighed in happy resignation. "You know I'll support you, whatever you say."

"I know. Really, the kids are great. Jesse's ear infection cleared up, and Gracie is growing like a little weed."

Just then Jesse came running through the house with his diaper in hand and its contents spilling on the floor.

"What am I doing wrong?" she lamented into the phone. "Here comes Jesse with his diaper off, leaving a trail for me to clean up. I guess I'd better go. I love you. We'll talk soon. Maybe we can go to lunch later this week."

Anne barely heard her grandmother's reply as she hung up the phone and went after Jesse. "Stop, right this minute," she yelled as she chased a giggling Jesse down the hall. *Why didn't I ask Granny how she potty trained nine kids and lived to tell about it?*

Catching her energetic toddler with one hand while clinging to the baby with the other hand wasn't an easy task. Now she had to figure out how to get everyone clean and supper on the table by six o'clock. Her husband, Jack, had been out of town on business, and she'd promised him a home-cooked meal on his return. She wanted to tell him it would be much easier if he brought home pizza, but he never quite understood how busy her days were. Those few lines she got to read in her novel constituted the only break she'd had the entire day.

Looking at her watch, she realized it was already four thirty and time was running out. *What do I have in the freezer*, she thought as she scrubbed the wood floor for the third time that day. *Maybe the ham is still in there from Christmas. I could thaw it in the microwave . . .*

The phone rang again. Anne got up from her knees and made her way into the kitchen once again. *I'm too old for this.*

"Hello," she answered, trying to sound more pleasant than she felt.

"Hi, honey! How's your day going? It's really been busy at the office. I got back in around noon, and you know how hard it is to play catch-up."

Anne stood with a Lysol can in one hand and a mop in the other as she listened to her husband's cheerful voice. "Same here," she managed to say. "Just as busy as little bees!"

"Great," Jack chirped. "I can't wait to see you guys. I hope you don't mind, but since you were cooking tonight anyway, I asked Donnie from accounting to come for dinner. We've been trying to get together on that project for a week now, and I figured tonight's as good a night as any."

Anne's silence spoke volumes, but Jack didn't notice. "Are you still there? Can you hear me?"

"I'm here. What time did you want to eat?" Anne's voice was as frosty as an old freezer.

"I was thinking we would come a little early so we don't have to work too late," Jack replied, seemingly oblivious to his wife's dilemma. "How about five-thirty? He's single, so don't worry too much about the house. He'll just be happy for a home-cooked meal."

"Great, see you soon." Anne put the phone rather firmly in its cradle and added sarcastically, "Oh, you mean he won't mind a little mess on the floor as long as I have some good food?"

She finished cleaning the hallway and went to the laundry room to put away her cleaning supplies. *I will remain calm . . . I will remain calm . . .* she began chanting in her head.

The sound of splashing water caught her attention, and she bolted into the bathroom to find Gracie tottering over the toilet, the water just within her reach, having the time of her life.

"Oh, Gracie, no, no. The potty isn't a toy." But Gracie didn't agree and managed one more splash before Anne whisked her away.

Anne sat Gracie on the bathroom counter and lathered her down with soap. Gracie dangled her little feet in the sink, finding another new game to play.

As she watched her daughter in the mirror, Anne couldn't resist smiling at the chubby little face and beautiful brown eyes looking back at her. Her hair was soaked and formed one little curl on her forehead.

"Okay, you are adorable, but your daddy is expecting dinner in forty-five minutes, and I haven't even started!"

"Come on, you little monkey. Let's get some clean clothes on you, and then I have to think about supper."

Anne smoothed baby lotion on Gracie, put pajamas on her, and placed her in the highchair with a handful of Cheerios on the tray. "There, now you'll stay out of trouble for a while. I'm not so sure about your brother."

She headed back down the hall to check on Jesse, but before she reached his bedroom, the doorbell rang. Anne sighed, rolling her eyes in despair. "What now?" She peeked in Jesse's room, not wanting him to see her, and was thrilled to see that he was still quietly playing. She tip-toed backward and then headed for the front door. "If this is a vacuum-cleaner salesman, I will not be responsible for my actions," she warned no one in particular.

"Granny, what are you doing here?" Anne exclaimed, surprised at this unexpected visit. "Come in!"

"We didn't get to finish our conversation earlier, so I decided to come on over anyway." Anne's mouth dropped opened as she watched her grandmother waltz past with her hands full of potholders and saucepans. "I fixed your family some dinner. I called to tell you, but those babies were keeping you too busy to listen. Anyway, when your grandpa was alive, he used to say, 'Don't ask if you can help, just go ahead and do it.' So here I am. I hope you don't mind. If you've already made something, you can just save this for tomorrow. There's nothing here that won't keep."

Anne was speechless. *How could she know?* Her eyes welled up with tears of relief and gratitude as she hugged her grandmother. "Granny, you will never know how much I needed this tonight," she whispered.

"Oh, I think I already do. I'm not too old to remember—been there, done that!"

They shared a good laugh and, arm in arm, headed to the car to unload the rest of the dinner.

# Facing the Unknown

*Chapter Six*

When you face the unknown, seek Me and I'll answer you, delivering you from all your fears. When you look to Me, you'll shine. Come to Me with all your worries, because I care deeply for you. Find the secret of being joyful in hope, patient in trouble, and faithful in prayer.

Guiding you,
Your God of Hope

—from Psalm 34:4–5; 1 Peter 5:7; Romans 12:12

*Contemplating the future* can be fun, but sometimes it can also be frightening. Years ago explorers made their way over treacherous mountains or through dangerous woodlands to secure their future family homes. They were willing to risk their very lives to guarantee a better future for their children and grandchildren.

Times have changed, and we rarely have to risk our lives to make sure of our future. Still, the uncertainty of where our future might take us can be scary. Generations have gone before you, but you'll need to make your own mark on the world. You probably won't be called on to forge your way through the wilderness, but

you still must navigate the rough terrain of
choices that will determine the course of your
life.

Daunting, isn't it? You may wonder if you're ready
to forge ahead into the unknown.

You are.

You've watched those who have gone before you.
Their experience has been your training. It's never
easy to accept responsibility, to realize that others
are now looking to you as the pioneer who will
clear a path for them. But, Granddaughter,
face the future with confidence, knowing
that you are loved. That you will always
be in our hearts. That whatever life
demands, you can do it.

*Every experience
God gives us,
every person He puts
in our lives, is the
perfect preparation
for the future
that only He can see.*

♦

Corrie ten Boom

The left turn into the
driveway nearly took
her breath away
as she realized how
unprepared she was
for this moment.

# love remembers

The short one-hour trip from Alexandria to Natchitoches, Louisiana, felt instead like a tedious cross-country journey. Kaitlyn's eyelids were leaden from lack of sleep, but her heart was even heavier. She blinked hard to try to bring some moisture back into her tired eyes and struggled to think of something besides Grandma and Grandpa Jones.

It was no use. She couldn't help reliving the many trips she had taken to that house. She thought of the big family van, coloring books, markers, sticker activities, and tiny cars strewn about on the floor. Her mom had tried everything to keep sibling squabbles to a minimum. Eagerly anticipating a week or weekend of Grandma's good cooking and Grandpa's fishing trips, Kaitlyn and her brothers could hardly contain their energy and excitement.

Even now she could almost smell bacon frying and Grandma's homemade biscuits, fresh and hot. "You can just pick them up with your fingers and sop them in the syrup," her grandma would tell them. Kaitlyn's mouth watered involuntarily at the most delicious memory of all, the wonderful scent of fresh pecan pie wafting from the oven. She sighed, weighed down with the knowledge that she would never experience days like that again.

She looked right and left to cross an intersection and became conscious of how much the landscape had changed in the thirty years she'd been traveling this small, two-lane highway. The trees were bigger, the gas stations more frequent, and the traffic heavier. *Everything changes*.

Her parents had gone to the house the day before, but Kaitlyn couldn't get off work until the weekend. Her brothers would come when they could get free from jobs and other obligations. But as the oldest grandchild and the only girl, Kaitlyn always felt more responsible for helping out.

She turned on the radio to the local Christian station, looking for some comfort. A remix of "I Come to the Garden Alone" was playing, and soon Kaitlyn's eyes were full of tears as she thought of her grandmother's sweet voice singing with the other fifty or so church members on Sundays. No megachurch for her grandmother. "I don't need a lot of folks around me to know I'm doing the right thing," her grandma had told her once. "I just need me and the Lord to worship." Kaitlyn smiled. Her grandmother's dedicated faith had influenced their whole family.

A pothole jarred her to attention, and she realized she was almost to the water tower. "I see it." "I saw it first!" "You didn't call it!" She could hear echoes of the van full of kids arguing about who saw the tower first. They all knew it meant they were just minutes away from Grandma's house.

Natchitoches was the oldest city in the Louisiana Purchase. One downtown street was still made of the original bricks. The Cane River meandered right down the center of the sleepy little town. Kaitlyn's brothers would line up on the riverbank, fishing with Grandpa, while she and her grandmother wiled away the hours browsing in antique stores and eating ice cream. Most of their evenings were spent the same way each trip, frying the fish the boys had caught and laughing about how many hooks Grandpa had to get out of a tree or a floating limb.

Kaitlyn turned right automatically and admired the row of pecan trees that always welcomed her to Grandma's house. *No wonder she baked so many pecan pies.* She breathed in deeply, pretending to get a whiff of a pie cooling on the kitchen counter.

She slowed down as if to take in every sight and sound Watson Lane held that day. *It's the end of an era.* Three children were playing basketball, and two more were riding bikes. A young man was loading up his boat with an ice chest and fishing gear. A young mother was pushing a toddler in a fancy stroller with cup holders, and an older woman walked briskly down the street with her back to Kaitlyn.

*Grandma's neighbors . . . I wonder if they know. Some of them probably do. Others may be surprised when the* FOR SALE *sign goes up.*

The left turn into the driveway nearly took her breath away. She suddenly realized how unprepared she was for this moment. Her grandmother's house without her grandmother. It just didn't seem right.

Even though Grandma had been sick for five years, Grandpa had always taken care of her. Now the disease had progressed, and he was tired. He had called Kaitlyn's mother and said he was ready to move in with her and to put Grandma in a nursing home. It would be better, they all agreed. None of the family lived in Natchitoches, and it was hard for Kaitlyn's mom to check on her elderly parents. With the move back to Alexandria, they would all be able to see each other more often. Today was moving day.

Kaitlyn put the car in park, closed her eyes, and said a prayer for her family as they bid farewell to a house and a life they loved. She walked to the front door, trying to avoid stepping on the pecans that dotted her path. She glanced toward the carport, half expecting the fish fryer to be sending up steam. It wasn't.

The screen door squeaked and squawked as she opened it.

"Well, there you are, honey," her grandpa said from his favorite chair.

Kaitlyn smiled at him, always amazed at how he had stayed the same sweet man in spite of the difficult years of caring for a wife with Alzheimer's. "Hi, Grandpa. How's Grandma doing?"

"She's about the same. She's in her bed." He grew a little somber. "Kaity, she may not recognize you this time, but remember she loves you just the same."

"I know, Gramps. I'll never forget that." Kaitlyn swallowed the lump in her throat and hugged him tightly. "I can't wait to see her. Where's Mom and Dad?"

"Packing up the bedroom. Your mother sent me out here to take a break."

Kaitlyn wished the hallway could be as long as it had seemed when she was younger, but instead it felt shorter than ever. In just a few steps she could see her grandmother staring out the window.

"Hi, Grandma!" She tried to sound cheerful. Her grandmother turned her head as if she was ready to acknowledge the person speaking, but no words came. Kaitlyn sat on the bed beside her.

"Grandma, it's Kaity." She took her grandmother's hand and started the one-sided conversation. "I just got here. It was a beautiful drive over this morning." Searching for words, she added, "Are you looking at those nice pecan trees in the yard?" Kaitlyn watched as her grandma tried unsuccessfully to fit the pieces together. Finally, with a wrinkled brow and a faraway look, her grandmother managed a weak "Hello." It was all Kaitlyn could do to not break down and cry.

"Kaitlyn," her mother called from the guest bedroom. "Come on in here. We have so much to show you."

Kaitlyn kissed her grandma on the forehead and said she'd be right back. She crossed the hall and found her mom and dad knee-deep in memorabilia. School pictures, coloring pages from Sunday-school lessons, old letters, and an assortment of homemade crafts covered the bed and much of the floor.

"Hey, Mom and Dad," Kaitlyn said as she hugged both her parents. "Mom, it's too hard. How are you getting through this?" She picked up a photo of herself and Grandma with their Easter bonnets on. She just stared at the photo, unable to speak.

"Kaitlyn, it is hard. You're right. We're so caught up in the memories, we can hardly pack. But we're making a little progress. I wanted you to see these things in case we don't unpack them for a while. Someone else in our family needs to know what treasures will be stored in these plastic bins." Kaitlyn was impressed at how neatly her mom was preserving the family mementos.

Her grandfather joined them and surveyed the room with a sweet but heavy sigh. "Kaity, your grandmother loved you kids so much. Just look around this room and you'll see that she always wanted you near her. If she couldn't be at a school play or ball game, she'd have your mother save some item for her so she could feel as though she'd been there. When she got to go, she always brought something back to remind her of the good time she'd had.

"But she also left something for you. A few years ago, before her memory got too bad, she wrote each of you kids a letter. I've saved them until now. Your grandma knew this time would come, but she was prepared." He handed a letter to Kaitlyn.

Her hands shook as she opened it, and she had to wipe tears from her eyes in order to make out the writing.

*Dear Kaity,*

*I remember standing outside the hospital nursery, watching you wiggle your mouth to form that same dimple your mother has. I think your grandpa had to pry me away after an hour of just staring at you. From that first moment on, I have never been disappointed in you. You have brought nothing but joy to my life.*

*I know you're sad that I'm not with you as I used to be. But dearest Kaity, while I may be silent on the outside, inside I'm full of memories of you. Look in every drawer and every closet of this house and you'll see evidence of the memories I've tucked away.*

*I know you're there taking care of me and your grandpa, and I want to thank you for loving us and allowing us to share your life. One more thing— look in the kitchen drawer beside the telephone and get that recipe for pecan pie. I know you can make them just as good as mine!*

*I love you forever,*
*Grandma*

Tears spilled down Kaitlyn's cheeks as she dissolved into her mother's comforting embrace. Soon they were all holding on to each other in the tiny bedroom on Watson Lane.

"Well," Grandpa said, clearing his throat. "I'm hungry."

Kaitlyn looked down at the letter she still held. "Grandpa, let's go find that recipe. What this house needs is the smell of a fresh pecan pie."

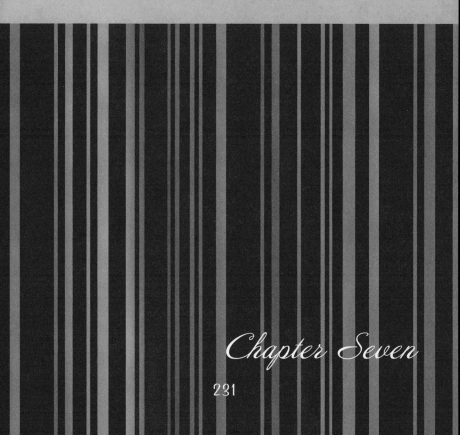

# Continuing the Legacy

*Chapter Seven*

231

*Let My love compel you. Living a legacy of love is the excellent way! Share with others what they need. Let My statutes be your heritage and the joy of your heart. As you live every day, set your heart on following My instructions.*

Blessing you,
**Your Creator**

—from 2 Corinthians 5:14; 1 Corinthians 13:13;
Romans 12:13; Psalm 119:111–112

*You sit beside them* on a riverbank, sharing a fishing pole. You stand on a stool beside them, patting down biscuit dough. You lounge on the back porch with them as you watch frogs play on a hot summer day. You think you're just having a fun day. But what you don't realize is how much joy you're bringing to some of the people who love you most—your grandparents.

Watching a granddaughter laugh and play is one of a grandparent's favorite pastimes. But sharing with her the many valuable lessons we've gained throughout our lives ranks among the most rewarding activities too. Some people say God gave us grandchildren so we could make up for everything we forgot to teach our own children. But that's not really true. It's just that we love you so much we want to do everything we can to equip, inspire, and encourage you to thrive, to make a difference, to leave a legacy.

So thank you for your patience when we seem determined to teach you everything we know. Thanks for spending time with us and for letting us share our hearts with you. For being our best legacy. We couldn't be more proud.

One thing, and only one,
in this world has eternity
stamped upon it. Feelings
pass; resolves and thoughts
pass; opinions change.
What you have done
lasts—lasts in you.
Through ages, through
eternity, what you have
done for Christ, that,
and only that, you are.

◆

F. W. Robertson

"It smells funny. Why do I have to go?" Alicia had pleaded as a child. Now she was glad she'd gone.

# cookie day

The smell of freshly baked cookies filled the kitchen as Alicia looked under the table for her daughter's missing shoe. "Come on, sweetie," she yelled from an upside-down position, grabbing the missing shoe with one hand and balancing herself with the other. "The cookies are almost ready. You know how Granny looks forward to this day and will be waiting for us."

She looked up just as five-year-old Amy came running into the kitchen with an armload of dolls. "Mommy, can I take my new Barbies to show Granny? She might want to play with them." The energetic youngster, one shoe on and one shoe off, was peeking through blond and brunette Barbie dolls—two dressed in fancy gowns and two more in the latest sports clothes.

"Sure. Granny will love to see your dolls. Let's get your shoe on, then you can put your dolls in your backpack." Alicia reached down to pick up Amy and set her on the kitchen table, at a more adult-friendly shoe-tying height. "I'll put the cookies in a plastic box. Then we'll be ready to go."

Amy jumped down and ran to the back of the house, pigtails bouncing. Alicia smiled as she thought of how much joy Amy had brought to Granny.

Her grandmother had only been in the nursing home for three months. She was adjusting well, but Alicia knew how important the visits from family and friends were to her. It was her grandmother who had taught her the biblical principle of caring for those who are "shut in."

*It's still hard to believe these trips are now to visit my grandmother instead of going with her to visit others,* Alicia thought as she scooped cookies into a plastic container. She shook her head in lingering disbelief. *The same nursing home where she's spent years ministering to the occupants . . . I should be picking her up to go with me, not going to see her there.*

Alicia had only been two years old when her grandmother started including her in her shut-in ministry. Once a week they would bake cookies and head to the nursing home to encourage the patients who lived there. It was clear to Alicia even then that the senior citizens loved seeing someone young, and for many years she loved being the center of attention. But as she got older, Alicia had found the trips less pleasant and had begged her mother to let her stay home.

"Mom, it smells funny. Why do I have to go?" she would plead. *So much complaining about doing such a simple act of kindness*, she thought now.

"Honey, it's so important to your grandmother," her mom had answered. "You'll be glad once you go." That hadn't always been true then, but now she was glad she had gone. She cherished the heritage of love her grandmother had handed down to her and was grateful for the opportunity to hand that down to her own daughter.

"Mommy, I'm ready." Amy pulled at Alicia's jeans, trying to get her attention.

Alicia patted her on the head. "I am too. Let's go."

Once they were on their way, Amy began her usual chattering and asking questions. "Mommy, why does Granny live with all those other people?"

"Remember, I told you Granny is a little sick now, and your Grandma Parker can't take care of her anymore. She needs a nurse to take care of her." Alicia thought of her mother's struggle as she had made the difficult decision to put her own mother in a nursing home.

"Oh, I forgot." Amy seemed satisfied with that simple explanation. Alicia looked in the rearview mirror to see her daughter's contented face. She glanced up at herself in the mirror and noticed that she didn't look quite as peaceful. But she knew the truth—that her grandmother was more than "a little" sick. Her chronic lung disease had progressed so that she suffered from frequent bouts of pneumonia. It was a condition she had lived with for years, but at eighty-eight years old, her body was tiring of the fight.

"Mommy, tell me about when you were little and would go to the nursing home with Granny." Amy had asked to hear the familiar story over and over again.

"Okay, but you've heard this story so many times. Aren't you tired of it?"

"Nope," Amy responded from the backseat.

"Well, when I was little, every Tuesday morning at nine forty-five, Granny would pick me up to go to the nursing home with her. She always brought homemade cookies, carefully stacked in a shoe box, for me to pass out to her friends. I would hold the box on my lap as we drove and try to not eat them all before we got there." Alicia let out a little giggle at the memory. "Of course, I couldn't resist at least one. And Granny would make sure she had enough so I could eat one on the way. It was always the same kind of cookie—a tea cake. She said her friends didn't need a lot of sugar, and those didn't have much sugar in them."

"Did they like that kind?"

"You bet. It's the same kind we make when we have time—like we did this morning." Alicia picked up the story again. "In those days, kids didn't have to sit in car safety seats, so I sat right next to Granny. If she had to stop quickly, she'd reach over really fast and hold me back with her arm." She added softly, almost to herself, "I always felt safe with Granny."

Alicia smiled and could almost feel the comfort of snuggling next to her grandmother. "We would sing all the way to the nursing home. 'Jesus Loves Me' and 'Victory in Jesus' were our favorites. Once we got there, Granny would open the door and waltz in like she was famous, and her friends would be waiting for her. Some were in wheelchairs, some were in beds in their rooms, some would be watching TV on the couches. But they all knew who she was and were happy to see her."

"Just like when we go. Right, Mommy?"

Alicia looked again in the mirror to see her daughter grinning. "Just like when we go," she affirmed with a smile. "You know, it makes Granny very happy that we're continuing what she started."

Amy didn't respond, and Alicia glanced back to see a concerned look on her daughter's face.

"Mommy, who will do this when I go to kindergarten?" School would be starting in two weeks.

"You know, I've been thinking about that. When I was little, Granny went every Tuesday morning—I only went with her in the summer. But since Granny is there now, maybe we could change our cookie day to Tuesday afternoon, after school. How does that sound?"

"I like that idea," Amy responded. "I don't want to stop seeing Granny."

Soon Alicia and Amy arrived at Plantation Manor. Armed with a box of cookies and a backpack full of Barbies, the cookie team swung open the door, ready to make someone's day brighter. Alicia looked around for her grandmother, but she wasn't in her usual waiting spot in the foyer. Alicia approached the nurse's station, trying not to sound alarmed, in spite of the sudden knot in her stomach. "Good morning," she said, "I didn't see my grandmother, Mrs. Hacker. Do you know if she's in her room?"

The nurse looked down at Amy and back at Alicia. The deliberate eye contact was all Alicia needed to tell her things were not right.

"Good morning, Alicia."

Alicia could tell the thoughtful nurse was keeping her tone light to protect Amy.

"We called you and your mother, but you had apparently already left. Your grandmother had a bit of a rough night. She's running a little fever, and the doctor would like to put her in the hospital."

Alicia took a deep breath as she absorbed this new information.

"Mommy, let's go see Granny." Amy was tugging at Alicia's leg again, not comprehending the reason for the delay. "She's probably waiting for us to pass out our cookies."

Alicia spoke again to the nurse, asking more with her eyes than she could with her words. "Should we go on in to see her?"

"I think so," the nurse responded. "She's just resting until the ambulance comes to take her to the hospital."

Amy squatted down to meet her eager daughter at eye level. "Amy, Granny's not feeling well today. She won't be able to walk around with us as we deliver the cookies. The doctor is going to take her to the hospital so she can get better and come back to help us. We can go see her, but we have to be a little quieter than usual. Okay?"

"Okay."

"Okay, let's go." Alicia turned and headed toward her grandmother's room, but Amy took off in the opposite direction.

"Whoa, missy," Alicia gently grabbed her daughter's arm and tickled her stomach. "Granny's room is this way."

"But what about the cookies? Everyone's waiting for them and for us to go and make them smile."

Alicia caught her breath as she looked at her innocent but thoughtful daughter. *Just like Granny—she'd be so proud.* Her throat clenched as she tried to hold back emotions her little girl wouldn't yet understand. "You're right, Amy." She swallowed hard. "Let's pass some out on the way to Granny's room."

Amy giggled as she took the cookie box from her mom and headed toward an older woman in a wheelchair. Alicia could barely hold back her tears as she watched a legacy in action. Amy opened the box, took out a cookie, and handed it to the woman. "Do you know Granny?" Alicia heard Amy say. "She lives here now. She taught my mommy how to make these cookies so we could bring you one. I hope you like it."

The woman's face brightened as she took the cookie and patted Amy on the head, and Alicia was taken back thirty years to the many times she'd had similar interactions. She remembered feeling the warmth of her grandmother's smile that communicated love and pride in her.

"See my backpack?" Alicia heard Amy tell her new friend. "My Barbies are in here. I'm going to leave one with Granny to keep her company when I have to go to school."

The wrinkled lady in the wheelchair had tears glistening in her eyes as she spoke softly to Amy. "I think your Granny will love to have a Barbie to keep her company. You are a very thoughtful granddaughter." She reached out to give Amy a hug. "Thank you for the cookie. You've made my day."

As Alicia watched Amy walk proudly back to her, she knew this was one tradition worth keeping.